TONY PULIS
HIS 40 YEARS IN FOOTBALL

DAVID LEE

Proverbial

First published in Great Britain in 2014 by

Proverbial (a subsidiary of LBA books)
www.impossibledreamers.co.uk
Stoke-on-Trent

All characters and events in this publication are actually quite real, so there's no real need to
mock them. Any confusion you may have with the long ball, the sweeper system, parking the
bus or the off-side rule is your own concern. Frankly, I've got better and more important
things to do with my…oh, look, some cake! Awesome!

Acknowledgments

Extracts From *Always Managing* by Harry Redknapp in Chapter 1: Published by Ebury
Reprinted by permission of The Random House Group Ltd

Extracts originally published in The Guardian that are used in Chapter 2
are reproduced with their consent

Selection of photos reproduced courtesy of The Sentinel

Many thanks to them and to Rob Ledgar, Mike Jay, Mick Cunningham, Robert Neesam,
Ross Hancock, Keith Wales (The Sentinel), and Martin Poole

Where possible, permission for reproducing material has been sought, and we thank the
many generous people and organisations who have allowed us to use this material.
Apologies to any organisation that we've somehow missed or we were just unable to trace.
Most interviews conducted by author. Reported press interviews reproduced in good faith.
Furthermore, we have striven to ensure that all is factual, and hope that you agree that we
have been fair in our appraisal.

Special thanks to Shell and Dylan for the inspiration.

Foreword by Rory Delap

I remember when Tony Pulis signed me on loan from Sunderland in October 2006, he said he wanted to make it a permanent move in the January window. But there was no real agreement; we never even shook hands over it really. Then two games into the loan, I broke my leg, and there wasn't anything tying Stoke to honour the deal. Fortunately, the Gaffer and the club agreed to stand by their word to sign me. The way I was treated sent a message to others that Stoke looked after their players, something that often makes a difference when players are considering signing for a particular manager.

I'd never met him before then, but I'd heard about him from Danny [Higginbotham] and Ricardo [Fuller]. People had said that he could be hard to work for at times because he asks for EVERYTHING, but that's the sort of manager I think I work best under, and it proved to be the right decision. But then he too would also speak to players and listen to what they had to say about former colleagues. He even asked Danny and Ricardo about me to ensure he wasn't signing a bad egg! Later he asked my advice about lads like Liam Lawrence and Dean Whitehead to ensure they would fit in. He knew this could make or break team spirit, which is so much part of a team's success.

Promotion to the Premier League was a massive moment for us all, but he wasn't so happy when players were subsequently whisked away for photo-shoots and the like, which he saw as a bit of a distraction. He'd soon be there, telling you what he thought about it, and reminding you that you should be resting or preparing. With me he would be throwing in the age thing, "At your age, you should be resting!" he'd say with a smirk, but you knew he was serious. That usually meant I had a minute left to finish speaking with a journalist, or else.

He ran a tight ship, but I think that was a big part of his success. He always knew what was going on, when it was going on, who was up to what, which isn't an easy thing. But it worked for him and it worked for me, and you knew where you stood with him...particularly if you didn't go that extra yard!

Rory Delap
August 2014

Anthony Richard Pulis
Made in Wales, Constructed in Bristol

Chapter 1 – Tony Pulis the player (1974-94)

Part 1: The Rovers Years

It could have all been so different...

The date was Saturday 30th August 1975, the day of the Bristol derby at Ashton Gate. It was into this pit of 18,000 baying supporters that Rovers manager Don Megson decided to plunge the 17 year old tyke Anthony Pulis for his first team debut.

Like a true pro, Tony declared he was over the moon: "I remember Don told me I was playing on the Thursday and I was over the moon, but didn't really think about it being a derby match. Then as the game got nearer, the local press featured me and so did the TV but I wasn't particularly nervous."

Perhaps not nervous, but he did sound somewhat exuberant in the pre-match press: "Wow! What a debut! The boss has stuck his neck out for me & I've got to work my heart out to make sure I don't let him down!"

But would his little heart take it? "We drove into Ashton Gate on the afternoon of the match and as I passed the old Open End there was a sea of blue and white. The noise from the ground was unbelievable and it

Debut! The Pulis saga begins.
Megson sticks his neck out for Tony

was then I realised what it meant to Bristol, and to be honest the nerves kicked in. We had good old pros who were more than willing to look after a youngster from the Valleys – Frankie Prince [Rovers midfielder] being one of them. He told me I would be OK and to enjoy it."

Rovers took an early lead, but City equalised a quarter-hour later. Both sides missed chances, with Rovers taking most of the flak, saved only by the heroics of their goalkeeper, Jim Eadie, who apparently "flung himself around with the agility of a man half his size"(?).

With 15 minutes left and the game finely balanced at 1-1, Tony beat City's offside trap on a counter attack for a 1-on-1 with the goalkeeper. "I remember waiting for the linesman to call offside but it didn't happen, so I carried on and tried to lob it but it went wide." It would have given Rovers their first derby win for 12 years.

"Here I come" . . . says debut boy Tony Pulis as he leaps between Welsh team-mates Andrew Evans (left) and David Williams just after being told he will make his League debut for Rovers in tomorrow's big match against City at Ashton Gate.

He gets shock call-up for the big match

"When the game ended I was just relieved to have had a good game, and the lads were brilliant to me."

But how things could have been different if he had scored!

For one, he'd have been the hero of the hour, hoisted on shoulders and carried home on a sea of brown ale. His name would be up in lights - "Debutant Pulis seals Rovers victory in crucial Bristol derby!" would scream the local headlines - and the West Country pubs would echo his name for weeks, with young kids clamouring round him for an autograph as he got off the bus beside the gasworks. In years to come, Rovers fans would recount stories of where they were when Tony saw off the Cider Army in one of the warmest Augusts in history.

He'd have made a damn-sight more than 121 starts for Bristol Rovers in his 9 years there, and scored more than the modest 5 goals for them. And one thing's for sure: there was little chance that he would ever have become manager of Bristol **City** in 1999. In fact, not a chance in hell: rival fans have long memories.

But fate had a different course for Tony Pulis. After a 0-0 home debut against Charlton (a game Megson slammed as a "fiasco" and "our lowest ebb") he was dropped back to the youth and reserve teams. There he struggled for first team football for the next two seasons, as Rovers fought to avoid relegation from the second tier (now The Championship).

But what a way to start a footballing career.

"I think I'm lucky to have made it in a local derby. I had a good game. I found it really quick and a lot more physical than reserve games. The atmosphere that day certainly prepared me for the rest of my career."

The Man From The School Of Excellence

In July 1974 16-year-old Tony had crossed the River Severn to join the Bristol Rovers "School of Footballing Excellence" programme, transferring from his hometown team, Newport YMCA. At the time Rovers had a South Wales Youth policy (including a 'nursery' side called Clifton Vale) taking numerous youngsters from across the Severn Bridge. The deal was they got to play against Rovers' Under 14's and 15's sides, and if they were better than the Rovers' players (as Tony was) they were asked to join the club.

"I was spotted as a schoolboy by Rovers' legendary scouting network in Wales. People like Stan Montgomery, Bill Dodgin and Bobby Campbell were tremendous people to be around when learning your trade as a player. They instilled good habits in all us lads and Rovers were a great club to be part of."

It certainly was a great time to join as Rovers had just been promoted to the old Division 2 in 1974, and they were enjoying a 1970s golden era, although in reality this

Baby Tony shows off the plastic fork he was born with

involved several seasons fighting relegation. It was during his time at Rovers that Tony formed links with people who would play a big part in his future.

The manager was Don Megson, father of Gary Megson (later a coach with Tony). John Rudge (later Stoke's Director Of Football) was a Rovers striker. Paul Hendrie, father of Lee Hendrie (a key Stoke loan-signing), played in midfield. Chic Bates (later a Stoke coach and manager) was a striker. David Williams (later Tony's assistant manager at Bournemouth) was a midfielder. And then a young Ian Holloway joined a star-studded Rovers team of England internationals that featured Alan Ball, Terry Cooper, Gary Mabbutt, Mick Channon and Bobby Gould. There was even a young welsh player called Mark Hughes (no, not THAT Mark Hughes, but in fact Emlyn Hughes' cousin).

Most significantly was the senior defender Lindsay Parsons, senior in the sense that the full-back had been with Rovers since 1961. After more than 350 appearances for the club, he moved to Torquay in 1977, but

Gently stepping over the keeper, Tony headed home

would be back in touch with Tony in the 1990s as his assistant manager, before going on to be a coach and scout with him for two decades.

And there were many more ex-Rovers players/coaches that would pop up in Tony's timeline, particularly at Stoke City: Mark O'Connor (coach) Gary Penrice (European scout), and Gerry Francis (First Team coach).

Although the 1970s were exciting times at the club, Tony didn't really become a regular until manager Megson left and Bobby Campbell (a former Rovers player) took over in late 1977. Inheriting a struggling team – they'd just lost 0-9 and 1-5 in consecutive away league games under Megson – Campbell needed some steel in midfield. Matters came to a head for the FA Cup 3rd Round game at Sunderland. Campbell picked Tony, and the team won an inspiring 1-0 victory at Roker Park despite being reduced to 10 men. Tony Pulis was a regular after that. He later claimed it was his most memorable game.

Tony was a fiery 5ft 10in player who could slot his tough-tackling skills – such as they were – into defence or midfield. In fact it was manager Campbell and coach Harold Jarman who converted the defender to playing in midfield. Tony thus became a "vital figure in the side", keeping the club afloat in the 2nd tier with the help of the prolific Paul Randall banging in the goals [Randall disappeared to help Stoke gain promotion under Alan Durban in 1979, before returning to Rovers soon after.]

Tony Starts A Riot!

Tony never scored many goals, only 9 in his whole career. But one strike he can brag about was the cracker he scored against Chelsea.

It was the 23rd February 1980 when a high-flying Chelsea side visited Eastville for a league game, bringing with them a huge following for Rover's biggest game of the season. Over 14,000 filled into the ground, over twice the normal gate. Two goals by Shaun Penny (either side of half-time) had effectively sealed victory for Rovers. Then Tony stepped forward and hit a 25 yard screamer into the net for 3-0.

The atmosphere, already incendiary, went off the Richter scale, with the whole stadium going crazy.

"Our third goal," a Rovers fan recently recollected "was a brilliant goal by Tony Pulis. The best goal I have *ever* seen live". Even a sympathetic Chelsea fan wrote to Rovers after the game wishing them well in their fight against relegation: "No doubt the two points against my team, not to mention an excellent third goal, will go a long way to help you in that course."

Teenagers, eh?!

Tony was modestly less impressed with the goal, jokingly describing it as "a miss-hit". However, he had to admit later that it was the best goal of his career.

Unfortunately, whilst the home supporters went mad with delight, Tony's goal was just too much for the travelling fans. It was the spark that began a riot amongst the disgruntled Blues supporters, who first of all tried spilling past police on to the pitch (amazingly only one person got through). "Our third goal was too much for them to bear," said Rovers chairman Graham Holmes. "They intended to force the referee to abandon the game." Instead they rioted down the streets of Bristol, smashing windows, looting and attacking cars. The story made the national news, with 35 people taken to hospital, and 30 arrests. In court, even the prosecutor, Rosaleen Collins, declared that "The worst incident happened when Rovers scored the third goal, and all hell let loose" proving conclusively that Tony's goal had sparked the insurrection.

There aren't many Premier League managers who can claim they've ever scored a league goal against Chelsea; even fewer who can claim it was an amazing strike; but probably only one who can claim that it also started a riot.

Tony falls dramatically against Aston Villa but...is it a penalty?

Tony Escapes The Rovers Relegation

But there was also unease behind the scenes at Rovers, particularly when former England full-back Terry Cooper moved from Bristol City to Rovers to become player/coach, causing a dressing room split between Cooper and Campbell/Jarman. Eventually when Cooper became player-manager in 1980, the wheels on the bus fell off altogether. Rovers sank quickly to the bottom and stayed there, only winning ONE in their first 29 games of the 1980/81 season. Rovers finished bottom of Division 2 with only 23 points, with rivals Bristol City going down with them.

In truth, Tony had little to do with Bristol Rovers' relegation in April 1981. He actually left in January to play abroad. But one thing he did learn was that a club could only succeed if everyone was pulling in the same direction. He had passionately backed Campbell and Jarman, and so soon fell out with Cooper when Terry became manager. Tony thus only starting 6 league games at the beginning of what became Rover's "holocaust" season, before being sent to languish in the reserves. But it is still recorded (unfairly) as the only time that Tony has ever been relegated, despite him only being a squad member early on. He swore that he never wanted to experience it again. He also learnt that if you fall out with the manager, he may never play you again, however good you are and however hard you work.

At just 23, Tony had a difficult decision to make when a club called Happy Valley showed him interest: "I was at Bristol Rovers and I had a difference of opinion with the manager, Terry Cooper. Then Ron Wylie [former-Villa & Coventry coach] called and made me a fantastic offer to go to Hong Kong. It was enough for me to put down a deposit on our first house. Me and Debs were about to get married. No way would we have been able to afford it otherwise. So it was a big chance. It was also a big gamble with my career. At first, I thought I'd made a mistake. But the club really looked after me and I played with Charlie George. And in the end, I went straight back to Bristol Rovers anyway."

It was certainly a lucrative offer, and the tax-breaks were, to say the least, considerable. The players were well looked after, often with luxury apartments, and a good time could be had, if you could cope with the weather, food and the 7am training sessions. Tony being a grafter, soon fitted in. The standard of play was a lot lower than he was used to ("It compared to the standard of Division Three, with attendances between 3000 and 30,000"), but he always believed in giving 100%. "There were only 16 teams, yet they had five cup competitions every season, as well as their league. There was always a good chance you would win something. We finished 2nd in the League and won one of the Cup Competitions. Overall, I had a great year. They were a good club and every Christmas Happy Valley still send me a Christmas card."

He also got to rub shoulders with the likes of Tommy Hutchison, Charlie George, Bobby Moore and Dave Jones. Even Stoke's Terry Conroy played out there around that time.

When ex-pats met up, they used to exchange stories. One was that if the score was 0-0 at half-time, the chairman might appear offering more bonus money to go on and win. The Chinese players soon cottoning on: "Keep score down till half-time," they'd say, "then boss panic and more money!"

Another story involved manager Ron Wylie's 80-year-old mother-in-law, who insisted on being introduced to Bobby Moore at a Hong Kong social gathering just so that she could ask, "Bobby, did you really nick that bracelet?"

The Rovers Return

Tony returned to Bristol Rovers in late 1982 and joined Bobby Gould's star studded (albeit 3rd Division) side featuring Alan Ball, Mick Channon and the emerging Ian Holloway. But it wasn't easy.

Bobby Gould's backroom team at Bristol Rovers. Tony adrift on the right

"We learned our trade at a football club with really, really good people who had old fashioned values. I truly believe that it's because of the way we were brought up back then that we have managed to go on and achieve what we have done in the game. The basic principles were drilled into us, both on and off the pitch. Nothing was given to us and we had to work very, very hard for everything we got."

Tony also returned as youth coach, but it was not universally popular. As striker Paul Randall put it, "I was not so pleased as Tony was a fitness nut. I knew that we would be in for a few cross-country runs in training." But he did consider Tony to be an "excellent coach. He encouraged me and told me I was working hard for the team."

Tony in the meantime was taking full advantage of learning from the old pros, particularly Alan Ball: "Bally was brilliant, a great lad. Alan was about 37, but he was the best one-two touch player I'd ever played with. He was unbelievable. Later, I took over from him at Portsmouth. I went round and seen him and asked him about the place." [It was Alan Ball's last managerial job. Portsmouth had been heading for relegation before Tony took over.]

Young Rovers striker Errington Kelly remembered Tony as "a very enthusiastic and knowledgeable coach; a real football person, who really knew what he was talking about, even in those early coaching days. I think he'd picked up a slight injury, so he wasn't playing that often in the first team."

Tony was a quick learner. Before he'd even become a regular first teamer, he utilised an eight-month ankle injury lay-off to obtain his first FA coaching badges when he was only 19, followed swiftly by his UEFA 'A' Licence by the age of 21 – one of the youngest pros to gain the qualification. It was not always so popular to do so.

"Bill Dodgin senior [Rovers manager before Don Megson] – one of the shining lights in my football life – was still at Rovers then. He had been the manager of Sampdoria, but when he found out I had been on a coaching course, he slaughtered me.

"He thought coaches were a hindrance. He just believed in a pure game. So he thought it was really wrong for a young kid to be doing it. I never regretted it, apart from the rollocking he gave me."

Errington and Tony

Ravenous for knowledge, Pulis went on courses at Lilleshall alongside Dave Sexton, Don Howe, Bobby Robson and Terry Venables. He even visited France studying academies, something Arsene Wenger might have been surprised to learn.

Homecoming

With the team revitalised by Tony's return, Bobby Gould's all-star Rovers side finished 7th. But despite David Williams taking over from Gould, the club just failed to gain promotion the following year, ending the season 5th. Tony described it as one of the most disappointing moments of his playing career.

The sort of crap Tony had to put up with: studs in the shin and karate chops

So in 1984 Tony decided to trek back over the Severn to join Newport County, close to where he had been born. It gave him the opportunity (initially) to play more as the tough-tackling midfielder than defender. The £8,000 transfer also had other advantages: he got to work with ambitious manager Colin Addison (formerly at Derby); his younger brother was a reserve striker there for a short time, and his father in law, Bill Stroud, had played wing-half for County in the 1950s; and he didn't even have to move home from his Bristol house 10 minutes from Eastville. Also, an ex-Newport player Dave Williams (no relation to David), whom Pulis had admired when watching County as a boy, was now the club's coach, and clearly someone whom Tony could relate to. "I can remember him putting a few wingers over the touchline!" Tony reminisced soon after joining.

It didn't seem such a bad idea at the time – Newport had been in the quarter-finals of the UEFA Cup Winners Cup only 3 years previously. But after only one season (finishing a disappointing 18th, 5 places lower than the previous season, & losing 8 of their last 9 games) Addison left to work in Qatar. Tony became disillusioned with a club now on a downhill path to financial oblivion. "We had a good decent side, but I could see many administrative problems; behind the scenes there was no organisation." The club would go out of business completely in 1989. Moreover, Addison's successor, Bobby Smith, turned out not to be Tony's cup of tea. He'd formerly been Port Vale's manager for a short period, where he'd spent big money but still got relegated.

Tony's career appeared to be, in the immortal words of Ozzy Osbourne, "going nowhere fast".

Monsters vs Animals

Tony once described himself as "A very average player, but a player all the same! I worked my socks off to make something of myself. When I left Newport on the train at 16 to go to Bristol Rovers I told myself then that I was never going back to that life. I thought this is my chance and I wanted to take it."

David Williams recalled: "Tony would be the first to admit he wasn't gifted as a player, but he made the most of what he had. He was hard and had a competitive streak in him, and even at that age he wouldn't

Tony reduced to playing in the car park

tolerate anybody in a team that wasn't prepared to be the same way."

His style of play is best remembered by John Rudge as being "combative and dependable".

Rudge: "He was a strong midfield player, very competitive, liked to tackle. He was not what you would call a technical player."

However, that wasn't the whole story.

When Harry Redknapp later signed him for Bournemouth his then quote to the local rag was "Pulis is one of the hardest men in the

Division, so we will be very hard to beat." A year or two later he looked back on the reasons why Pulis was the man for him: "I felt we needed more steel in the squad. Tony was a tough competitor and added some bite to us in midfield. I knew he could do a job for us."

Cherries fan & author Robert Neesam wrote at the time of Tony's reputation: "One thing is for sure; while I had not yet observed recent-

signing Tony Pulis in action, all the talk about his reputation as a hard man meant that I already feared him. His character appeared to be similar to 'Animal' from The Muppet Show, an individual who would let actions speak louder than words. He had been elevated to the status of a rough and tough western gun fighter. Thank goodness he was on our side!" As Robert later observed, Cherries fans soon referred to Tony as 'Iron Man'.

Harry's Game

But if you were under any illusion as to what type of player Tony was, you only had to look at Harry Redknapp's autobiography,

Harry Redknapp: "When he set off for a tackle you wanted to dial 999"

"Always Managing". After only one cursory mention in his previous 1998 autobiography "Arry", H went to town on his Sandbanks neighbour in his 2013 memoir:

"He was a monster, Tony - the toughest tackler I have ever seen."

And Harry went on...

"He wasn't a stylish footballer, but he made it bloody hard for those that were. You hear legendary stories about Ron Harris and Tommy Smith these days, but Tony would be up there with any of them when it came to the hard stuff."

...and on...

"Some of his stunts were unbelievable. We had our own tough nut, Keith Williams...hard as anybody, a wicked tackler, he always did a great job for us. I didn't know Tony Pulis from Adam, but 10 minutes in he had sorted out Keith like nothing I had ever seen. He'd come in quick, sharp as a razor."

...and, er, on...

"He couldn't actually play. He couldn't pass it more than five yards, really, but when he set off for a tackle you wanted to dial 999 just to be on the safe side."

...and on and on and...

"Tony retired from playing to become part of my backroom staff. I'm sure most of the league breathed a sign of relief when that happened."

...and...

"And players would get away with it in those days...but back then I'd rather have a lad like Tony in midfield for me than against me."

A lot of it was tongue in cheek. Harry may have thought Tony a tough tackler, but certainly not nasty. He saved his vitriol for the crazy-gang Wimbledon team of the 1980s, and his particular disgust for one of their defenders: "I wouldn't have Vinnie Jones here [at Bournemouth] for anything. He is a thug in football boots and sets a terrible example. He sickens me more than anything else in the game!" So maybe Tony wasn't so much a monster.

Everybody Was Kung Fu Fighting

Not everyone shared Harry's sentiments, and Tony clearly had a few more strings to his bow. An example being the story of Roy "Red Card

Roy claimed in his book that after the foul, he walked straight off, not even waiting for his red card, yet here he is still on the pitch (right) as Tony receives treatment

Roy" McDonough (the big angry striker infamous for his record-breaking 22 red cards) who took umbrage with Tony if only for being diminutive and gobbie. For 90 minutes, Tony wound Roy up rotten, but wisely kept out of the wild man's reach. By the end of the game the exasperated Roy, then with Cambridge, admitted he "wanted to kill him"!

The following year, Roy's Southend played host to Tony's Newport in the FA Cup, with McDonough seething for revenge. It took only 7 minutes. In an attempt to emulate Bruce Lee, Roy tried to drop-kick Tony kung-fu style. Further, Roy said that as he landed he "tried to finish the job by messing up his head with my studs" but Tony was just too fast for him. Unsurprisingly, Roy was red-carded again, ruining any chance his club had of a lucrative cup run.

Exchanges were keen and O'Keefe was booked following a foul on Pulis. Then it was the Rovers player who was in further trouble for, having already been cautioned, he wrestled Hunter off the ball and was promptly dismissed in 40 minutes.

Half-time:—

PORT VALE 1
BRISTOL ROVERS 0

Despite saying he was gutted to have let his manager Bobby Moore down, Roy somehow reached the conclusion that the fine, the ban, the cup defeat, and the betrayal of his manager's faith were "worth the crime". Tony just got up and carried on. Newport won 1-0, and had their own lucrative cup run, which was only thwarted at Sunderland by 0-2.

Setting an example

But that was after his first coaching job in charge of Rovers' youth team when Bobby Gould was boss. A combative player, Tony brought the same principles to the training ground, as Geraint Williams (then a Rovers defender, now the Wales Under-21 manager) discovered: "I upset Gouldy for some reason one day and got sent to train with the kids. After about five minutes one of the first year YTS boys 'topped' me, and I grabbed him by the neck. Tony shouted: 'Put him down, I've only just taught him how to do that'."

Gould remembers: "Tony was the slowest runner I ever saw. A good tackler, mind, and a fantastic football brain. I saw a lot of myself in him. The same passion for the game. People look and think you are a raving loony, but when players who have got talent work with those sort of people then they realise they are being taught how to make the most of their gifts."

But despite his tough-guy image, his discipline was surprisingly

18

impressive. In his 8 years with Bristol Rovers he was only sent off once. Ironically it was at Port Vale in September 1983, where he was dismissed after a second bookable offence before half time for "wrestling Geoff Hunter off the ball". It was ironic as his ex-colleague John Rudge was Vale's assistant manager (although probably away scouting as he has no recollection of the event). More ironic, being Rovers' Youth Coach, Tony probably wasn't setting a good example there. Rovers, who'd been 0-1 down, went on to lose 0-2.

After Rudge became manager, Tony returned to Vale Park with Bournemouth, this time winning 2-1. However, it was also memorable for Tony as he sliced a clearance into his own net. He was never much keen on Port Vale after that.

Part 2: The Bournemouth Years

When Harry met Tony

On a typically miserable rainy day in 1986, a down-on-his-luck football manager drove cross-country to run an eye over an obscure hard-tackling midfielder in a game being played in South Wales. The rest, as they say, is history...

The story of how Tony Pulis teamed up with Harry Redknapp is now the stuff of legends.

Here were two figures whose careers really were drifting, with their futures far from certain.

Harry was a former West Ham and Bournemouth player, who was taking his first tentative steps in management at Bournemouth, after succeeding Don Megson (coincidently Tony's ex-Rovers boss) in 1983. "H" had overseen three relatively mundane seasons with them in Division Three, finishing 17th, 10th and 15th . He'd tried offering up attractive football, but had little to show for it, although he had managed to knock Manchester United out of the cup, and won the very first Football League/Autoglass/JohnsonsPaint Trophy, although the cup final venue was curiously switched to Hull, and played out in front of only 6500 fans. [It's a long story involving The Horse Of The Year show. Just don't ask.]

Harry may have been relatively popular in the Boscombe area, but he was hardly setting Dorset alight, let alone the world.

As his third season began to drift into lower-midtable mundaneness, Harry decided that what his side needed was more backbone, a more physical presence on the pitch. It was time to toughen up if his side was going to progress.

His first thoughts were to the player who had turned over Harry's own hard-man last time they'd played. This was the player who was going to change things at Dean Court. His name was Tony Pulis, and his career also seemed to be going nowhere fast (or "the lower divisions" as they're sometimes called).

As the Notts County defenders beg for mercy, Tony shoots...again

It was Friday 28th February 1986, and Newport County were playing Walsall in a 7.30 kick-off. Ironically, County and Harry's Bournemouth side were both on 35 points at the lower end of Division 3, despite Bournemouth having the league's top-scorer, Colin Clarke (24 goals). [Interestingly, Bournemouth's goal-difference was a superior 44-48 compared to Newport's stingy 30-35. The Pulis-factor was in evidence even then!]

However, Harry reckoned Tony Pulis was worth another look. So, as he was heading north anyway for Bournemouth's game at Darlington the following day, he decided to make a detour to take in more of the Pulis-experience.

It had been a dreadful winter, one of the worst since 1947. Snow had blighted the football programme, and now the thaw and persistent rain were hitting clubs hard. There was even talk of Darlington, having played so few home matches, running out of money to pay its players before Bournemouth even reached them on the Saturday!

Harry decided to face that hurdle when he came to it. In the meantime he continued on his rain-drenched drive to Somerton Park in his battered old Morris Marina. As he drove, there was news of more and more fixtures being called off at Plymouth, Swindon, Brighton, Reading, West Brom, etc. etc... The weather became so bad that the pools panel had to sit again the following day to adjudicate the results of all the cancelled games. [They gave Stoke an away win at Palace!] Harry began to wonder if the Newport game was going to be on at all.

After a long arduous journey, fighting his way through waterlogged roads and the Friday night rush-hour traffic, Harry finally arrived at the ground, just 10 minutes before kick-off. He staggered in and plonked himself down in the tea-bar used by the football scouts before the game, which was little more than a small wooden hut. As he looked around his eyes fell on the last person he expected to see there: Tony Pulis. Tony wasn't playing – he'd been dropped. Harry couldn't believe it.

Fighting off Brian May from Queen,
Tony shoots and scores

But the football world would never be the same!

As they watched the game together, Tony bemoaned the fact that he hadn't been picked, unhappy with how the manager was running the club. He certainly seemed vindicated: Newport were slaughtered that night, losing 5-1 in front of their home crowd, their worst home defeat in years.

Harry was impressed by what he heard, and it seemed that Newport were nothing without Tony. He drove off for his own game the following day at Darlington. He'd got no money to sign Tony, but he had learnt that Tony would be available on a free transfer at the end of the season anyway.

As the 1986 season came to an end, Harry sold his international star-striker, Colin Clarke, to neighbours Southampton and used the money to build a promotion winning side, of which Tony Pulis formed a key part.

Tony's first promotion

1986/87 was Tony's most memorable season as a player, and was all the more remarkable for Bournemouth. After seeing off Newport (ironically) in their first home game by 2-1, they were soon scrapping for top spot with the likes of Bruce Rioch's Middlesbrough (just relegated), Lou Macari's Swindon (just promoted) and Terry Cooper's Bristol City (just not happening).

Tony often displayed a suave sophisticated side to his playing style

Boro were the main threat. Just back from administration, they were on a march that would lead them to the top flight by 1988. But Bournemouth only really faltered when Tony picked up an injury in November – they lost 5 of the 6 games that he missed. When he returned they went on an unbeaten run of 12 (in fact, only losing 1 game in 18), although teaming up with the new signing, defender John Williams from Vale, also helped.

Curiously (bearing in mind his shyness away from home as a manager) Tony was boosted by the announcement in October of his new kit sponsors: The AFC Away Travellers. They had selflessly held a series of social evenings and raffles to raise the £200 necessary to sponsor him. For that famous 100% effort, he was clearly appreciated by the away supporters. Would that this was always the case.

He was also appreciated by home supporters, particularly when he miraculously managed to overturn a referee's decision to give a goal against Bournemouth. In a game against Walsall, the linesman indicated a foul had been committed just before The Saddlers equalised, but the referee seemed oblivious to the brief wave of the flag. Tony was incensed almost dragging the ref over to the lineman from the centre-circle. After a brief discussion on the touchline, the goal was amazingly disallowed, and The Cherries went on to win 1-0. In those days, it seems, Tony had more influence over refereeing decisions.

What was there not to like?

After a historic 3-1 victory over Middlesbrough in March 1987, Bournemouth were unstoppable. Promotion was sealed on May 4th at an emotional game at Craven Cottage. They had effectively come from nowhere (well, east Dorset) to become champions of the Third Division with a club record 97 points, promoted to the Second Division (now The Championship) for the very first time in their history. For the record, Newport (by now in administration) finished rock bottom and were relegated. You'd either got it, or you didn't. In this case, it was the Pulis-factor, and The Cherries had got it.

Popping Off To Gillingham

In Bournemouth's first season in the old Second Division (1987/88), Tony played a vital part in ensuring the club stayed up, as they finished 17th (of 24). He even popped up and scored the occasional goal, in fact 3 in a whole season, his highest ever tally. But then he suffered a pre-season injury, and when he finally fought his way back into the side he was sent off in a 1-0 home defeat against lowly Shrewsbury in October 1988. (It was no consolation that former Villa star David Geddis was also red carded after they clashed in midfield.) As is often the case, the team went on a successful run (finishing 12th) and Tony was reduced to only 10 appearances that season.

A famous footballing mogul,
and some guy who used to play for Spurs

Gillingham and Huddersfield were keen to take him on loan before the 1988/89 season finished, but Redknapp was reluctant to part with him. However, after receiving offers from Aldershot, Brighton, and Maidstone, Tony accepted a £10,000 move east along the coast to Gillingham, just relegated to Division 4. Their new manager swung the deal for Tony. "Damien [Richardson] impressed me greatly and persuaded me to come here in much the same way that H persuaded me to join Bournemouth," he said, soon after joining. The prospect of being the focal point of a new sweeper system didn't bother him either. "Playing a sweeper need not be a negative move, especially if you end up playing with only three men at the back." Even for Tony, these seemed like positive intensions.

But the move turned out not to be such a good idea...not for Tony nor for AFC. He suffered another pre-season injury, originally believed to be a torn thigh muscle. But when he broke down in a reserve game two months later, it turned out to be worse than first thought.

"Unfortunately the pre-season did not go as planned as I broke a bone in my leg during a friendly with West Ham. My first appearance for The Gills came just after Christmas when we put together a good little run. One problem was I was trying to sell my house in Ringwood

[Hampshire], and it was a bad time as the market had dropped. I found travelling to and from Kent a bind, but if we'd have been able to move, I would have definitely served my three year contract at Gillingham."

Tony's first four games brought four straight wins, and as the 1989/90 season progressed, Gillingham rose to 3rd, before falling back to finish mid-table. Tony only managed 17 appearances. It was worse for Redknapp's Bournemouth who struggled badly after Christmas. With a thin squad, and defenders in short supply, the club crashed to a last day relegation in front of rioting Leeds supporters. They certainly went out with a bang – Stoke City finishing bottom was sedate in comparison.

After working so well together, Harry Redknapp and Tony Pulis were finding life difficult working apart, and their futures suddenly seemed uncertain. Tony was now 32 and had studied a Small Business Course with Mark O'Connor to give him options in case football

NOT THE 8502
92 - 93

AN AFC BOURNEMOUTH FANZINE

TONY PULIS'S

LILAC AND GREEN ARMY

ISSUE 26   SEPT/OCT 1992   60p

Lumbered with huge debts at Bournemouth, Tony was also burdened with a ghastly lilac & green strip

gave him up. Although Tony had got his coaching badges and done a little youth coaching, there was no certainty that there would be an opening for him when he finally hung up his boots. As for Harry, he had the tough job of turning Bournemouth around.

With the club in crisis, Harry called up Tony, persuading him to return for a £15,000 fee as player and first team coach. "He knew I hadn't moved to Kent, and I was obviously happy to go back and work with him." But as Tony prepared for his Bournemouth return, Harry was in a serious car accident in the summer of 1990.

With Harry sidelined for several months, Tony did his best to compensate with his coaching and motivation. "When I arrived the first thing I noticed was the lack of confidence among the players. They soon overcame that following some good results." Not long after Harry's recovery, Tony became his assistant manager, where he learnt a painful lesson: "I was mad on coaching and H would let me get on with it, but he would say, 'You can spend hours and hours out there, but if they don't take it in, Tone, you've got no chance. They have to be good players. Good players make the right decisions at the right time when the heat is on.'"

But then Harry seemed to know everything about every player around. "I learnt a lot from Harry. We used to travel up the motorway and I would get the Rothmans [Football Yearbook] out. He would be driving and he'd say, 'Pick a player'. I'd say, 'N Jones', and he'd be off, how old he was, who he played for, left-sided or right-sided, good in the air or not. The thing he taught me was that the players are the products, and if you have good products you will be successful."

> **Pulis's order to play more of a passing game took its effect three minutes into the second half.**
>
> *...& was concluded two minutes later*

But relegation and the accident weighed heavy on Harry, and with no sight of re-promotion, the club began to struggle financially as well as on the pitch. With another season ebbing away, Tony declared, "We're the nearly men, not good enough." At the time, Tony was being touted as Gerry Francis' replacement at none-other-than Bristol Rovers, whereas Harry was being eyed up by Stoke and Southampton.

In 1992, it all came to a head. After one behind-the-scene row too many, Harry was off, on course to coach West Ham, which was no surprise to anyone, except perhaps himself. Although his heart had always been in the Bournemouth job, even the press had to admit that H had often been a "loose cannon".

The Big Boss Man In Flip-flops

By now the club were 'relaxed' about Harry leaving, and even the normally forgiving fans were disgruntled with him for subsequently claiming bonus money from his contract, particularly with the club in dire straits. [The affair became known as 'HarryGate'.]

However, the incoming Bournemouth chairman Norman Hayward got on well with Tony, and they shared the same vision. Tony was into coaching, fitness and discipline. He was also willing to do all this on a tight budget, which would be paramount judging by the financial precipice that the previous administration had left behind. (The club had lost nearly a £1m alone in the previous 12 months.)

His appointment might not have been what supporters had wanted, as names like Luther Blissett, Kevin Bond and Jimmy Case were bandied around. But after Redknapp had recommended Tony, the Board moved swiftly to interview him. As Tony remembers, "Harry told me he was resigning and then said he was recommending that I should take over. I wasn't so sure at first. I asked him to stay for 6 more months, but he was adamant."

Tony had been holidaying in Florida. On his flight back to meet the board, his plane was struck by lightning, but it didn't put him off his stroke.

"The interview was set up so quickly that I turned up in the boardroom to meet the directors wearing just a t-shirt, shorts and flip-flops! But I told them my plans and hopes for this club. Harry had been a great influence on me, and I'd learnt so much from him, but I also had my own views on the job."

Bournemouth fanzine's view of behind the scenes

The directors, who'd originally wanted to advertise for a replacement, were impressed and offered Tony his first managerial job. Tony was delighted, telling the press, "We have earned a reputation for playing good football. I don't want that to change. I'm not for just lumping the ball forward."

But he did have concerns. "I'm replacing the most popular manager this club has ever had and facing debts of £2.6 million – I must be daft!" he joked.

But it was no joke. Even the Board described Bournemouth's predicament as a "battle for survival", and for Tony's two years in charge, that's what it became. Even when Tony asked for a car to go scouting for players, all he got was a battered old maroon Vauxhall. On the way back from Runcorn with the Chairman late one night, the car burst into flames. Tony calmly got the extinguisher out and put it out, before getting back in and driving home. Even then he kept the car on the road for a couple more years.

He was able to develop a basic backroom team, including former Rovers colleague and manager David Williams. But with banks and liquidators constantly at the door, Tony had to buy low and sell high, whilst keeping Bournemouth afloat in the Third Division. "The club was bankrupt when Norman Haywood took over. We worked very hard to cut wages, sell the best players and just keep our heads above water. It had to be done, although a lot of supporters didn't realise that." Against the odds, he actually succeeded in this task, but it was at a cost.

Bournemouth's weird home strip sponsored by...Exchange & Mart!
The players' reactions were mixed to say the least.

In those two years he spent less than £400k, but brought in nearly £2.7million in transfer fees. For that, his 3rd tier side managed to finish safely in 17th spot twice in succession (after previously finishing 9th and 8th). Although he had to sell many decent players, he brought in many decent replacements. One of his first signings was a young Hartlepool forward called Steve Fletcher for £30,000. He would go on to play a record 700 games for Bournemouth.

Although Tony won Manager Of The Month in February 1993, when Bournemouth were flirting with a play-off position, supporters were soon bemoaning his direct style of football. He soon gained a reputation of signing big players. "There is a perception that I always like a big team. I can remember talking to [former football manager] Alec Stock when I was at Bournemouth. He used to say when his teams walked out he liked to see men, not boys." So he set about signing a remaindered 6ft 1in striker from the Premier's long-ball crazy gang, Wimbledon. His name was Steve Cotterill. The mould was formed.

But worse were the stories of bust-ups with players that leaked to the press. It gave him good reason to move them on, although not always for optimum prices. There was even a fracas outside the dressing-room with a midfielder, who reportedly needed stitches, resulting in the directors having to step in. Tony naturally dismissed it: "It's a man's game. Maybe he hit himself on a door or something after I had gone." Finally, he even fell out with the local newspaper, which of course did him no favours, leading to a siege-like atmosphere.

His other problems included a transfer embargo imposed by The Football League, long-term injuries to key players (such as popular Steve Cotterill), lack of training facilities (they'd be forever phoning up parks and schools to find a surface to train on), and staff & players going unpaid for weeks. But disgruntled fans were unimpressed.

What did for Tony in the end was the familiar story of a new consortium taking over the club, not to mention attendances dipping in the final months of his second season. In reply to some fans claiming they would not return until Tony was gone, he retorted, "Empty vessels always make louder noises. I'm more interested in giving success to genuine fans." Some of these "genuine fans" wrote in, saying he should be given longer, like Harry was.

But he was not given the chance, and he left Bournemouth just before pre-season in August 1994 with a "mutual consent" payout for the remaining year of his 3 year contract. Without Haywood and Tony the club plunged towards financial oblivion, before eventual revival in the new millennium.

Although hit hard, Tony learnt quickly to be philosophical about the managerial merry-go-round. "When I first took the job as manager at Bournemouth, the club trainer Kirkie said to me 'You NOW will find out what management is about. You don't until you sit in the chair.' You can prepare and sit in a classroom for years and years, but until you get the job and get moving that's the only time you understand it. When I got sacked, I was absolutely devastated, and the first phonecall I got was from [fellow manager] Jim Smith who said 'You're not a proper manager until you've been sacked 3 times, mate!'"

Chapter 2 - The Long Road To Stoke (1994-02)

Part 1 – That Most Evil & Despicable Man!

On June 29th 1995, a young retired millionaire called Paul Scally bought a struggling 4th tier football club for £1. Some sceptics say that – knowing him – he wouldn't have paid that much for it (it was later

Paul Scally wondering if this was all such a good idea

reported that it only cost him one penny). Whichever sum it was, it was clear that Gillingham FC had got themselves into a lot of trouble. But after buying 87% of the club shares, Scally took the club out of administration literally hours before the liquidators came a-knocking and before they got thrown out by the Football League ("They were less than helpful," he growled).

Describing the place as "a derelict khazi when I arrived" (he was an infamous man of words), Scally proceeded to throw out the old brown carpets, the grubby net-curtains, the pre-50s décor, and the "moaning" tea-ladies (who weren't impressed). He replaced them with a new training ground and a new sponsor. But first he needed a new manager. Paul Scally wanted a no-nonsense football manager who knew how to work miracles on a tight budget.

Scally was working closely with Gillingham's previous owner Tony Smith, who'd remained friends with Tony Pulis from when he'd been at Priestfields as a player. When Scally wanted someone to assess the club's players a few months before he bought the club in early 1995, Smith recommended Tony, who'd anyway been brought in to do the same job for the receivers. Tony Pulis wasn't that impressed by the set of young players who'd "never really been taught how to play the game...as they'd never had the senior pros around to help them."

But after leaving Bournemouth in 1994, Tony had wisely spent months checking out players who might be available for his next project.

So when an impressed Scally offered him the job, he was ready to hit the floor running, which was just as well as he was only given a month to assemble and prepare a squad, mainly from free-transfers.

Ten months after leaving AFC Bournemouth, Tony Pulis was back in business, and back in Kent after 5 years away. What he found was a behind the scenes renovation, with 'wet paint' signs propped up against the doors as a small army of brush-yielding Gills fans helped spruce up the place. Change was clearly afoot. But in order to turn things around on the pitch he would need help, particularly from someone he could trust. So he called his old Bristol Rovers colleague, Lindsay Parsons.

Lindsay had been manager of Cheltenham Town for 3 years, finishing 2nd in the Southern League in all 3 seasons. But frustratingly only the champions were promoted to the Conference. [Ironically, when Steve Cotterill took over Cheltenham with many of Lindsay's players, they also finished 2nd, but DID get promoted because champions Gresley's ground failed to meet Conference standards. What are the odds?]

Lindsay Parsons (top) wondering if this was all such a good idea

Tony and Lindsay were an odd combination. As Lindsay admitted, they rarely agreed on anything football-related. "I do regret leaving Cheltenham in some ways because I miss having the final say, and I miss a lot of things about non-League football."

But one thing they did agree on was a revamp for the players. "I remember our first training session at Gillingham, and I told Tony the standard was far lower than what I had been used to at Cheltenham in the Southern League!"

It was at this training session at a local park where a man walked across their pitch and allowed his dog to crap right where they were playing. The group of players that Tony had persuaded to come to the club looked on aghast. "They were saying, 'This isn't the picture he painted'. I'll never forget it. It makes you appreciate where you've come from."

With Lindsay's help, Tony brought a freshness to training, with interesting new ideas and a training schedule tailored to each match. He made astute signings, like 6ft 4in striker Leo Fortune-West from Stevenage – very much the blueprint for a Pulis-player. Leo cost £5000, which supporters had raised the money for, and he repaid them by

Tony wondering if this shirt and tie look was such a good idea. Nope.

becoming top-scorer. In fact the only player that did cost any real money (£50k) was a former Gerry Francis protégé, Dennis Bailey. [Bailey is still famous today for being the last man to score a league hat-trick against Manchester United at Old Trafford in a 4-1 victory for QPR in 1992.]

Within literally a couple of weeks Gillingham were top of the league, with crowds suddenly doubling in size, completely filling the dilapidated Priestfield Stadium. In fact, 6 weeks in and games had to be delayed whilst fans crammed in through the turnstiles! Tony even won Manager Of The Month that September. It wasn't just a change; a revolution was happening.

It certainly helped that the manager and the chairman seemed to understand each other. After only several months, Scally was taking the longer view: "How can you build something if you keep sacking the manager? If you appoint a manager you should give him at least 5 years."

And astonishingly enough, after only one season, the club were promoted in 1996 as runners-up. They might even had been Champions but for a blip in form during March. But Scally was delighted – he'd supposedly backed Gillingham at 18-1 (a betting habit he would come to regret). Amazingly Tony's side had done all this scoring only 49 goals in 46 games – even Bolton scored 39 in 8 fewer games, and they'd finished bottom of the Premier League! Unsurprisingly perhaps, Gillingham had only conceded 20 goals – even Premier champions Manchester United conceded 35.

He did this in predictable Pulis style: "Tony is very dogmatic about organising his defence," said Steve Butler, who joined in mid-season. "He would call us strikers 'fancy dans' and concentrate on the defence. I have never seen a manager who was so good on the defensive side and in sorting out set-pieces. He had a captain, Dave Martin, who would run through walls for him."

Midfielder Neil Smith concurs: "Tony shook the club from the foundations, and it was exactly what was needed. I'd seen the club nearly go out of the league and out of existence. Having someone like Tony come in was like a breath of fresh air. It needed that shake up. Paul Scally also gave it a bit of an injection and direction. I can honestly say that I loved every minute of it. Training was hard work. I'd never trained like it before in all my career. Tony also brought us a belief. We went into games knowing we were going to win in the

Catching the bus to Division 2

tunnel. I would have run through a brick wall for Tony and the rest of the team because I know the other lads would do it for me."

Just as well there weren't many brick walls around.

In Search Of The Holy Grail

After winning Division 3 Manager Of The **Year** in 1996, Tony was suddenly in demand. After promotion, Tony had talks with Southampton, who were on the look out for a new manager to ease their Premier League struggles. Tony maintains he turned them down, and they weren't the only ones.

Instead his Gillingham team pressed for the Holy Grail, promotion to Division 1 (now The Championship) a place where the club had never gone before. In 1997 they finished 11th (of 24). But in 1998 they went on a late run of 12 post-Xmas wins to leave them needing 3 points in their last game to be sure of a play-off spot. Unfortunately, Tony was up against clubs backed by millionaires. Gillingham's last game was against Wigan (backed by Dave Whelan), who with Roberto Martinez and David Lee fought tooth and nail. Meanwhile, Fulham (backed by Al Fayed) were beaten by champions Watford (backed by Elton John) and so reliant on The Gills failing to win. Still having to sell his best players, it was no wonder Tony had a chip on his shoulder.

In the last minute, with the game 0-0, Gills sub Nicky Southall looped a shot from the edge of the box that hit the inside of the Wigan post. The ball was hit to safety, and the other scores began to come through. Bristol Rovers and Wrexham had both won against relegated sides (including Micky Adams' Brentford). Gillingham finished 8th, missing out on a play-off place by a whisker, on the old "goals-scored" rule. They were one of FOUR clubs on 70 points, but Tony's side finished lowest having scored only 52 goals; above them were Wrexham (55 goals) despite Gillingham having a better goal-difference than them. It was a bitter blow for Tony to lose out for not scoring enough goals!

Ahh, they were once such good chums. Tony, Pauly and Lindsay

Amazingly for a Tony Pulis side, the following year Gillingham increased their tally by an incredible 50% to 75 goals, even outgunning Manchester City, who finished one place above them in 3rd.

It was around this time that he started wearing the famous Tony Pulis cap, but it wasn't really for practical reasons. As he recalls, "I think it's more superstition that anything else. I started wearing it at Gillingham, and did very well there. It's just the fact that my career has not been too bad, so I'll keep on wearing it for evermore, I think."

But some of Tony's old habits he found harder to beat. He served a 28 day touchline ban, was fined for comments he made to referees, and he clashed with chairman Scally over investing in the team rather than the stadium. Scally in turn asked Tony to name him as a substitute in a game, just to win a bet...but unsurprisingly Tony refused (it was the last game of the promotion season). "The publicity has been fun, but I pick the team, and Paul knows the situation." Their relationship wasn't helped when the local paper misquoted Scally as saying that Tony had the "easiest" job in football, when in fact he'd said the "best" job. Furious, Scally ordered Tony not to speak to the paper, but Tony was less than compliant.

In November 1998, after getting a 0-0 draw at Maine Road, and beating 2nd place Fulham 1-0, Tony revealed that there were club payment problems: "There's a kid running around with a wage-slip £200 short." At the same time, a newspaper unhelpfully reported that Scally was talking to Micky Adams, the former Fulham manager.

Not helping his case, Tony mischievously observed: "Alec Stock once said, 'The difference is that there used to be gentlemen in boardrooms, now all I see is spivs.' I don't know. I never go into boardrooms." He would also continuously play the underdog, banging on about how Gillingham had the smallest squad in the league, and were on the lowest wages.

Nevertheless, towards the end of his time at the club, he was being tipped to take over from his old Rovers boss Bobby Gould as manager of Wales. As it was, the job went to a man with no previous managerial experience:..Mark Hughes. This might have been the turning point of his opinion of Hughes – when asked in 1987 what was the best goal he'd ever seen scored, he'd replied, "Mark Hughes' goal for Wales (v Spain)."

Gross Misconduct Down Tony's Shorts

But then in 1999, he and Scally fell out big-style. Scally sacked Tony for "gross misconduct" and accused him of trying to line up a job elsewhere while still managing Gillingham. Tony denied it and claimed he was owed a ton of money.

His departure from Gillingham in 1999 could fill a book (and would even make a good film). The subsequent court case that Tony brought against the club blew up out of all proportions. For those unconvinced, this is some of what The Guardian said at the time:

Tony just liked wearing shorts

"*The former Gillingham manager Tony Pulis was accused of concocting a "monstrous plot" to blackmail the club's chairman Paul Scally out of £200,000 using confidential documents stolen from the club, the high court heard yesterday.*

"*Pulis confronted Scally on May 26 1999, four days before the biggest game in the club's history, the Second Division play-off final against Manchester City, and demanded that the chairman pay him the money that Pulis was owed in goodwill payments, bonuses and his share of the sale of players.*

*"During the meeting, which took place in a stand at the Priestfield stadium, Pulis produced a document **from the front of his shorts** which, he alleged, showed financial irregularities. (He had put it there he said because he had no pockets).*

"Pulis, who denies the blackmail plot, also told Scally he would be leaving the club the day after the Wembley play-off, which Gillingham lost on penalties.

"In court, Pulis also denied accusing Scally of using club money to build an extension and swimming pool at his Kent home, and of buying cars for his wife and son and a Harley Davidson with club funds."

Yes, a touch more interesting than your everyday run-of-the-mill unfair-dismissal tribunal. Tony never did get all the money he felt he was owed, settling out of court late in the day (supposedly the £75,000 he was owed on his contract), when settling sooner might have been better all round.

What the case did do was to allow the pair to trade insults and air all manner of dirty washing in public. If that was their intention, well they certainly succeeded. By the end, even the media breathed a sigh of relief that it had finished.

It's only a game

Then there was that infamous play-off final at Wembley against none-other-than Manchester City.

The game had been fairly mundane until the Gills took the lead in the 81st minute, before going 2-0 up on 87 minutes! It was over, surely. A Tony Pulis defence wouldn't crack at this late stage? But crack it did. In the last minute, City pulled one back, and FIVE minutes into injury time, Paul Dickov slipped in the equaliser. Gillingham held firm in extra time, but fell apart for the penalties, only managing to score one, losing 1-3.

It was a bitter blow for Tony, and not an easy experience to get over, particularly as he was sacked soon after. "We didn't deserve to lose that game," he later revealed. "But it made me a much stronger person. You take things out of defeat as well as victory."

As for Scally, the *When Saturday Comes* magazine described him as a "laughing stock" when he appealed for the play-off final to be replayed after match referee Mark Halsey was allegedly seen drinking with Man City fans in his hotel following the game.

Even today Paul Scally hasn't got a good thing to say about Tony. Probably the friendliest gesture came a few years ago before Stoke played at Gillingham. Scally banned him from the ground...apart from the dressing-room, the tunnel and the pitch-side. But if anyone was in any doubt about his feelings towards Tony Pulis, it's fair to say that his description of him as *"the most evil, vindictive and malicious person I have ever met or worked with"* kind of sums it up.

As for Scally, he had plans to move to a new stadium, but instead he tore down the old main stand, almost as a statement of his rage towards Tony. Gillingham's inconvenienced fans saw them promoted the following season (mainly with Tony Pulis' team), but the success wasn't to last. Scally fell out with newspapers and fans, he was fined a record amount by the FA for betting on Gillingham's play-off final, the club was relegated all the way back to League 2, and then after overreaching itself the club hit the financial skids, with even the power being cut off due to unpaid bills.

But it was fair to say that Tony's career was also fairly chequered in the years that followed.

Part 2 - *Hiatus at Bristol City & Portsmouth*

Five days after leaving Gillingham, Tony was snapped up by Bristol City on July 5th 1999. City Chairman Scott Davidson, formerly keyboard player with Bros and The Pet Shop Boys (no, honestly he was), offered him a FIVE year contract (although later it was reported that he never actually signed it!), whilst gushing: "Tony Pulis is one of a new generation of up-and-coming managers."

A five year contract might have had something to do with the reason why he turned down Stoke City and Peter Coates at this juncture, as The Potters searched desperately to find someone who couldn't do a worse job than Brian Little. It was probably a wise move for Tony. Gary Megson, who did take the Stoke job, lasted only 4 months before the Icelandic consortium took over and brought in their own man anyway. It also explains why Tony was justified in describing Bristol City as the more "ambitious" of the two clubs. A *five* year contract?!

Naturally, as Tony had been with Rovers for almost a decade, Bristol City fans were not that pleased to see him. The fact that he also signed former Rovers striker Peter Beadle didn't help. But his skin was thickening to that sort of thing. He even had the nerve to stand up in their club annual meeting to say that City's players were "overrated, overpriced and overpaid here". He went on: "The club has been split with too many people wanting to build little empires and more concerned with their own well-being than that of the Club." He wasn't scared about knocking heads together.

The club were back in the third tier after only one season up in the Championship. It was hoped Tony could speed a quick return, but results were not promising. A 1-1 draw at The Britannia Stadium wasn't bad, but a 0-3 defeat at Gillingham was hard to stomach. A 0-0 draw

against neighbours Rovers (then top of the league) was fairly muted, only livened by Tony refusing to shake the hand of his opposite number, old friend Ian Holloway. (It was believed to be over a previous bitter game between Gillingham and Rovers.) Tony's team then spiralled downwards on a bad autumn run of 11 league games without a win.

But Tony's main problem was the supporters, although he took most of the flak in his stride: "I remember one training session it

Scott Davidson practicing his keyboards for Bros gig.
Ade Akinbiyi hides behind Tony. Lindsay Parsons
makes his feelings known using sign-language

was pouring with rain and my assistant Lindsay Parsons borrowed my red cap I always wore. The chief scout appears and says we need to go to the ground immediately. So we finish the session and go. We're greeted by two members of CID from Avon and Somerset constabulary. They told me they had received death threats about me and they had to take them seriously as they had mentioned my home address; they said they are watching me and see me about always wearing a red baseball cap. At that precise moment Lindsay took my hat off his head and put it on my head. We all fell about laughing, but obviously we had to take it seriously. I wasn't too bothered by a few nutters who told the police what they wanted to do to me. I always thought if you were serious you wouldn't tell the police anyway."

The mysterious case of Ade Akinbiyi

Although Tony was able to make a few signings, he felt he was undermined by the sale of Ade Akinbiyi. The Nigerian-capped striker had been nurtured by Tony at Gillingham, who had signed him for £250k from Norwich. But after a successful start there, Tony lost him to Bristol City for £1.2m. Finding him again on his arrival at Ashton Gate, Tony was non-plussed to lose him *again* when Akinbiyi was sold to Wolves for £3.5m only five games into the season. A month later he was still going on about it: "If we sell our leading scorer for £3.5m we need to go out and get someone else."

Tony's new skipper KeithMillen (caricature by Richard Mundy)

It was clear that it was going to take years to sort things out at Bristol City, particularly with a set of fans who weren't in the least bit interested in giving him a break. "I have to say there are some great people at City, and to be honest the supporters are passionate and there's nothing wrong with that. It was just one of those things at the time. It just didn't work out for both of us."

So when struggling Championship club Portsmouth started sniffing around Tony's ankles over Christmas, Bristol City supporters cheerily urged him to go. After overseeing a first round victory in the Auto-Windscreens competition (The Robins would make it all the way to the final where they would get beat by Stoke) he was tempted away after only 6 months in charge of Bristol to join Portsmouth on 14th January 2000. If the baying fans weren't persuasive enough, then the fact that Portsmouth was much nearer to his Bournemouth home and a division higher probably had a lot to do with it.

Initially the Bristol board cried foul, but when details of the five year contract were revealed, and the angry City supporters had had their say, the Directors were more receptive to Pompey's approach. Bristol City went on to finish an improved 9th, but it was several years before they were finally promoted. When Tony returned to Ashton Gate seven years later (with Stoke City) he was severely heckled by the home fans. In return, Tony wound home fans up further after the match by saying it "felt good to bring a team back wearing blue" (Bristol Rovers' colours).

However, the day after being appointed, Tony took charge of the Portsmouth team for the first time at Fratton Park. Pompey were 2-0 up in the first 25 minutes, and things were looking bright. But with a quarter of an hour to go Wolves began a comeback, miraculously making it 2-2 with just a few moments to go. Then in the very last minute a wayward shot was deflected in off a Wolves striker giving the visitors a 3-2 victory. The name of the striker? None other than Ade Akinbiyi.

Tony was shell-shocked. "When I saw his name on the teamsheet, I was disappointed.

The Ade Akinbiyi (right) being particularly mysterious in the game against Portsmouth

He's a player who can always score goals. He actually came in afterwards to apologise to me."

It would not be the last time their paths crossed.

Tony saves the day...er, again

On June 23rd 1999, a not-so-young millionaire called Milan Mandaric bought a struggling 2nd tier football club in a £5m deal taking them out of administration. (Haven't we heard this story before somewhere?) In a similar vein to the Paul Scally story at Gillingham, Mandaric began to look round for a no-nonsense manager to succeed Alan Ball, whose Portsmouth team continued to struggle into the autumn of 1999.

By the time Tony Pulis took over in January 2000 (on a three and a half year contract), Portsmouth were 22nd (of 24 teams) [not 23rd as Tony tells it!] after only winning 5 games in 26. In the final 20 games, Tony's side won 8, plus getting results against all of the top 4 teams, including a 1-1 draw at champions-in-waiting Charlton.

They even won 1-0 at 2nd place Ipswich, with one of many goals from striker Steve Claridge, who scored seven in seven matches. "Without his goals this season we would be struggling," Tony claimed. "His attitude has been first class. He leads by example." Tellingly, Claridge was less inclined to reciprocate the praise, later claiming to be unimpressed by Tony's tactics and training. This was particularly ironic as Tony was keen to give Claridge a good run in the team, after previous manager Alan Ball had remaindered him by telling the popular striker he had no future with the club. But under Tony, Claridge won Player Of The Year.

Most satisfying of all of Portsmouth's results was when they secured their place in The Championship with a point against promotion-pushing Manchester City, coming from 0-2 down to draw 2-2 late on, as City had done against Tony's Gillingham. Revenge was

Steve Claridge's best mate...not

sweet: Man City would have been all but promoted if they had won.

More Gross Misconduct

But after spending £4million on 10 players (including £1.25m for fragile ex-Vale striker Lee Mills) the 2000/01 season started poorly with only 3 wins in 15 games. "I'll just keep on doing what I do until someone else tells me otherwise," Tony said after a grim 1-1 draw at lowly Stockport in early October. Milan Mandaric gave him his "full support" to keep on doing what he did. Unfortunately, 24 hours later on 11th October 2000, he changed his mind and told him to stop doing it. In some way justifying the parting of the ways with his manager, Milan added, "I am not enjoying myself coming all the way from my home in Florida to places like Stockport and seeing us lucky to draw."

Intriguingly, Steve Claridge took over as player/manager, and the results initially improved. The dressing room was even described by one player as "a more joyous place now". But like a house built on sand, it didn't last, and the club started sinking again until it was back in 17th spot where Tony had left it. [Years later Claridge would blame his lack of success on a spate of subsequent injuries, suggesting that Tony's training methods may have somehow initiated them months before!?]

Despite all the rhetoric, it turned out that Tony Pulis hadn't actually been sacked. He'd actually been put on four months paid "gardening" leave by Portsmouth, supposedly to fight his bitter court case with

Gillingham. However, at the very end of December 2000, three months into this "leave", Mandaric cancelled Tony's contract for an alleged "misconduct".

Years later, Tony put his side: "He fired me for gross misconduct when there was no gross misconduct. It took 18 months to get to court and Portsmouth settled on the steps. It was difficult to take on Milan because he is a wealthy, powerful man. But it was a matter of principle."

Tony & Milan - what could possibly go wrong?

As for Pompey, they squeezed out Claridge after a miserable 2 wins in 20, and put Graham Rix (of all people) in charge in February 2001. As a result the club plummeted down the league, and had the indignity of only being saved from relegation by a win on the final day. Many thought even that was fortuitous, as it was their first win in 10 games. Their luck only changed when a certain Harry Redknapp took over in 2002, but then that's another story...

In The Court Of The Crimson Faces

Tony didn't work for two years between October 2000 and November 2002. It was a hell of a long time to be out of the game, and to compound that he had two gruesome court cases to deal with.

The first was the Gillingham/Scally case, which eventually came to court in April 2001, almost two years after Tony's sacking. It made harrowing listening as both mens' lives were hung out to dry...and then torn to shreds in open court. Both men were made to sound devious and desperate as they both fought fire with fire. It was not pretty.

At the time, with all the allegations of theft, blackmail and fraud (all denied), it seemed hard to be sympathetic to either side. However, when analysed in hindsight, Paul Scally has hardly helped himself over the years with his esoteric actions and antics, which many feel have undermined his credibility.

One of many examples of this was when Tony returned to Gillingham with Stoke in 2002. Scally was reported to have verbally attacked him, even encouraging the supporters to give him "the sort of reception he is entitled to". However, the supporters and the Gillingham team were loath to go down that road. Even The Gills' Player Of The Year Paul Smith told the press at the time, "Tony signed me from Brentford and the two years I had working with him were great. I love it at Gillingham, so I have a lot to thank him for."

This might not have been a smart move as Smith soon fell out with Scally over (would you believe it) money he claimed Gillingham/Scally owed him. So after receiving the Player Of The Year award for a record 4th time, Smith refused to hand back the trophy until they paid up. At least he didn't suddenly produce it from down his shorts! Unsurprisingly, Scally's Gillingham stubbornly dug their heals in and, well, just bought a new trophy. Just another typical day at Gillingham.

Even Adrian Pennock (later a coach at Stoke) fell out with Scally, claiming that he'd promised him a testimonial. "Over the ensuing two years I have been put off again and again by Mr Scally. Now we are not even speaking and I have taken that to mean the club does not intend to fulfil its agreement." A familiar story?

When the Gillingham case finally did come to an end on April 27th 2001, Tony Pulis saw very little of the £400,000 he was claiming for transfer bonuses, salary and benefits, settling instead for £75,000, said to be money in respect of the sale of Ade "that-man-again" Akinbiyi to Bristol City. There was also a matter of 'costs'.

Scally chose to pursue Bristol City and Stoke City for circa-£250,000 worth of legal costs which he claimed Gillingham had to incur to fight the Pulis court case. This, he said, was because the two clubs wouldn't initially admit that they had illegally approached Tony whilst he was still officially a Gillingham employee. [Tony had also spoken to Norwich around this time, but seemingly with Scally's permission.] The charges stuck against Bristol City at least, who had to pay Gillingham £50,000 in January 2003. With that, Paul Scally supposedly called time on the Pulis-feud: "That is the end of the matter because nothing more can be gained. Justice has been done, we've moved on and we don't like looking back." Would that it were true.

Meanwhile, Tony spent the next 18 months effectively preparing to take on Portsmouth and Milan Mandaric. The club resisted all the way, till finally on 29th October 2002 they reached a £400,000 settlement on the steps of the high court (although it was also reported as being £200k), over the fact that Tony had been sacked only 11 months into a 3 ½ year contract. Even this case had taken almost two years to settle.

The nightmare was finally over. What the 44 year old Tony Pulis needed was to get away from it all. Yeah, like that was going to happen.

Chapter 3 - Up Where The Air Is Clear (2002-05)

Part 1 – Life At Stoke

If Tony Pulis thought he'd had it hard, then he'd clearly never been a Stoke supporter.

"Now you will learn The Way Of The Pulis"

Just when they thought they'd seen as much despair and upheaval than any soul should have to endure – Stoke fans discovered they had to live through it all again.

After all, between 1989 and 1997, supporters had experienced a humiliating relegation to the third tier, a 3 year stint before eventual promotion, an Autoglass win, seven different managers, protests against the board, and struggling to come to terms with life in Division 1 (now the Championship).

So it came as some surprise in 1998 to find themselves going through the same drama again: humiliating relegation, a 4 year stint in the third, an AutoWindShield win, seven different managers, protests, and struggling in Division 1.

It was all getting a bit déjà-vu, with many fans wondering whether they were ever going to see the end of this topsy-turvy era.

The main differences between these two periods were the 1997 move to the breezy Britannia Stadium, which certainly didn't feel like home, and the 1999 arrival of the Icelandic Consortium, who certainly didn't feel like they fitted in, no matter how hard they tried.

If there was a turning point in Stoke's fortunes, it could probably be tracked back to the low-key and rather unusual appointment in 1999 of ex-Port Vale boss John Rudge as Director Of Football, overseeing activities behind the scenes. From the moment he arrived, the only way was up, slowly but surely. Despite a few rocky shoals, the good ship

Stoke City sailed a much steadier course with him on board. Much of the increasing stability that fans came to experience in the following years was down to Rudge, and the fact that he was ex-Bristol Rovers would play a large part in that.

The Managerial Merry-Go-Round

In the 1990s Stoke City had contracted the "manager-itis" virus – the symptoms being simply losing managers left-right-and-centre.

Thursday's paper - Burley behind "B***s up" sign?

As Oscar Wilde once wrote "To lose one parent may be regarded as a misfortune; to lose both looks like carelessness."

For Stoke City, Wilde would have quipped: "To lose one manager is a misfortune; to lose 12 in 13 years looks like plain stupidity."

In reality it was far worse than that. In fact, since Tony Waddington had walked out in 1977, Stoke City made TWENTY managerial changes in 21 years! Unbelievably, there were more to come, some just as daft.

Promotion to the 1st Division (now The Championship) had finally been secured for Stoke through the play-offs in May 2002. The Icelandic consortium decided that this was the ideal time (well, 4 days later) to part-company with manager Gudjon Thordarson, despite protests by thousands of supporters outside the ground.

Less than two weeks later, the board announced his successor from a three-man short-list consisting of Steve Coppell, Tony Pulis and Steve Cotterill.

Steve Coppell had just resigned from Brentford, whom Stoke had just defeated in the play-off final! He would go on to lead Reading into the Premier League.

Tony Pulis had been effectively out of the game for two years fighting court-cases. He would also go on to lead a club into the Premier League.

Steve Cotterill had taken Southern League side Cheltenham Town all the way to the Football League 2nd Division (now League 1) in 5 years! He would fast-track to the Premier League a lot faster than any of them.

Ironically Cotterill was a protégé of Tony Pulis. Tony – then manager of Bournemouth – had rescued the tall centre forward from then Premier League Wimbledon, where he had made only 24 appearances in 4 years. He became a firm favourite with Cherries' supporters, before a knee injury finished his career and he entered management.

Friday's paper - Tony searches for his season ticket

So it was a surprise (and perhaps ironic) that on May 27th 2002, at the age of only 37, Steve Cotterill got the three year contract at Stoke. Once the pupil, he now thought he was the master.

With the club hovering in the lower mid-table, things looked steady at Stoke, at least on the surface. But behind the scenes, Chairman Gunnar Gislason was calling for directors such as former chairman Peter Coates to resign, whilst Cotterill was increasingly frustrated at the lack of funds available.

Then, on 10th October 2002, after only 13 games, 3 wins, and 4½ months in charge of Stoke, Cotterill resigned to become assistant manager to Howard Wilkinson at Premier League strugglers, Sunderland. Everyone was aghast. Stoke fans immediately and rather poignantly christened him "Quitterill". It was quite a comedown; at Cheltenham he was known as "The Messiah Of Whaddon Road".

Whilst the clubs fought out a compensation deal for an illegal approach, first team coach Dave Kevan took over as caretaker. Curiously, Kevan had also been signed by Bournemouth's Tony Pulis, and like Cotterill had also had an injury there that had finished his career.

It was at this juncture that things went serious pear-shaped. As the board regrouped, struggling to bring in a manager, Kevan struggled with a deflated Stoke team, losing all 4 games that he was in charge for;

Wolves (0-2), Sheffield Utd (1-2), Rotherham (0-4), and Watford (1-2). Although they were all against top sides, it sent Stoke spiralling towards relegation.

Initially the board went back to their original short-list, but Steve Coppell had just become Brighton manager 3 days before Cotterill quit, and Tony Pulis was within days of finally reaching court over his Portsmouth contract.

Many big names were banded around in the press, including Bryan Robson, Peter Reid and Adrian Heath, although none of them were serious candidates. So as a result, Stoke fans were disappointed to learn that Tony was still favourite for the job. Many felt it was because he was a former teammate of John Rudge, but Rudge denied it, saying that he knew many people in the game: "Of all the applicants we had for the job this time I would say I knew about 40 of the people on the list, not just Tony."

The Oatcake capture the moment poignantly

But then there was a late entry. Respected manager George Burley had been sacked by Ipswich on the same day that Cotterill had quit, and the Stoke board suddenly put Burley at the top of their list. But they had to wait for him to return from a holiday in Tenerife, before they could invite him over to witness Stoke's home defeat against Watford on Wednesday 30th October. Although he was surprised not to see the same perky side that had recently beaten his Ipswich team 2-1 (effectively costing him his job), he talked after the game about ironing out contractual details. As a result, a press conference was booked for the following day to announce his appointment.

But overnight he seemed to think better of it, telling the board that he only wanted a contract till the end of the season. That didn't sound much like the commitment Stoke were looking for, and the press conference was cancelled at the last minute, much to the bewilderment of the media.

One theory put forward was that on the same night as the Watford defeat, Terry Yorath quit Sheffield Wednesday. Had Burley taken a phone call which might have changed his mind? Ironically a few days later it was reported that Burley was in talks with the Wednesday board. He didn't take the job, and would later manage Derby, Scotland, ...and even Crystal Palace.

Tony's task was a lot harder than he first thought (reckon The Oatcake's Gaz)

The timing for Tony Pulis could not have been better. On the Tuesday (29th Oct), the Portsmouth court case was settled, and on Thursday (30th) he got the call from Stoke and drove up from his Bournemouth home in his Ford Orion 1600 Ghia. The following day, Friday 1st November, he sat beside the Stoke Chairman as he was announced as the new manager of Stoke. Curiously, Gislason produced a nasal spray, complaining that journalists have an unreliable nose for a story. Then he left Tony in charge whilst he and directors flew back to Iceland. It was a bewildering start.

As for Cotterill and Wilkinson, they had a torrid time of it as Sunderland sank to the bottom of the Premier, finishing bottom with only 19 points. Subsequently, they were both sacked. Steve went on to manage a number of teams...including some of Tony's old haunts, Portsmouth and Bristol City. If they'd known he was a Pulis-protégé, might they have been so keen to hire him?

The other original candidate for the Stoke job, Steve Coppell, was also relegated that season with Brighton. Even Sheffield Wednesday, whom it was thought had tempted George Burley away, were relegated. With Stoke now down to 21st (of 24) it remained to be seen if Tony's side was also going down.

The Stoke City Shambles

Tony Pulis was recently asked what it was like at Stoke City when he arrived in 2002 compared to what it is today. There was a long pause, and then he took a deep breath. It was like he really didn't know where to start. Finally he said: "I walked into an absolute shambles!"

He wasn't wrong. As if the managerial shenanigans weren't bad enough, there was also boardroom civil war, continued wrangles about the council-owned stadium, a wholly inadequate team, a dysfunctional supporter base that had been further disenfranchised after Thordarson's dismissal, and there had even been a return to fighting on the terracing. He must have wondered why he'd bothered. However, Tony did see the bright side: "Putting the court-cases to the back of me was very pleasing. So, coming

"A New Era Dawns...Live The Dream" Eh?!

up to manage this football club was a delight for me."

Curiously, it had taken till he was 44 to get a job 'up-North'. Until now Tony had never worked for a club any further north than Gillingham in Kent! Suddenly he found himself in Stoke-on-Trent, a city transformed by the Clear Air Act, new industries like the up-and-coming Bet365, and a bright new (albeit half-empty) football stadium. What was there not to like?

Although he talked about moving nearer to Stoke, he and his family remained rooted in the Bournemouth area, with Tony living the life of a commuter. He would grow to be philosophical about this, particularly as

Before he meets the fans, Tony ensures he has adequate protection

he had stated when he was younger that the one thing he disliked most about football was "Long journeys back home after you've lost a game." He was going to get a lot of that to start with.

Stoke City may not have resolved many of their problems, but at least they were a division higher from when he had last been offered the job in 1999. As for Stoke's precarious position in the league, he stated that he'd never been relegated as a manager, and was determined to keep it that way.

So he played the standard Tony Pulis card: start by shoring up the defence to stop conceding so many goals. The problem was that for once it didn't seem to work, mainly because the players just weren't up to the task. Meanwhile, unimpressed Stoke fans, had been forewarned of his negative "direct football", all long-ball tactics and parking-the-bus. Word had it that he just signed big guys, who played rough, earning a load of red cards. It was also said that he lacked any charisma, which really was harsh. From the supporters' point of view, things couldn't get much worse, and they lay in wait.

They didn't have to wait long. Just after he joined, Tony met 300 disgruntled fans in the Waddington Suite at The Brit. As he approached the room, he asked John Rudge why there was so much noise coming from inside the suite. "Don't worry," Rudge told him, poker faced. "They're always like that before an execution."

His infamous first game as Stoke manager was at Walsall in the pouring rain, just 24 hours into the job. After the team leaked 3 second-half goals in 15 minutes, Tony had the nerve to take off crowd favourite

Bjarni Gudjonsson in a double substitution. The disgusted Stoke fans chanted, "You don't know what you're doing"...until his substitutes Andy Cooke and Chris Greenacre BOTH scored in the following 10 minutes, bringing the score back to 2-3. OK, they were both scruffy goals, but they all count. However, much to Tony's dismay, a late clumsily-conceded penalty ruined any chance of a comeback, and Stoke lost 2-4.

A rather damp Tony was left with no illusions as to how grim things were: "This will definitely be my hardest task because there is no money to spend. The ITV Digital problems [non-payment of money that had been promised to lower-league clubs] couldn't have come at a worse time. We've got to wheel and deal and get the best out of the players already here. When I took over Portsmouth they were several points adrift, but there was money and I was allowed to bring in 4 or 5 players. But John Rudge tells me the squad is actually weaker than at the end of last season."

Tony & Kevan at the Forest debacle

With the team already in a horrendous freefall before he'd even arrived, Stoke then lost their first four games under Tony, making it 8 in a row. Their first point was a 1-1 draw at Gillingham, the game where Paul Scally was offering such a luke-warm welcome. It took a further 5 games to even get a win, and that was against bottom side Sheffield Wednesday (3-2), with a last minute winner by Brynjar Gunnarsson. It was Stoke's worst run since their so-called 'holocaust' season (relegated from the top flight in 1985 with only 17 points).

But there were some stirring performances, particularly a 1-1 draw with league-leaders Portsmouth (by now managed by Tony's ex-boss Harry Redknapp), and a 0-0 draw at 2nd place Leicester (managed by ex-Stokie Micky Adams). Stoke even managed 0-0 draws at high-flying Wolves and Ipswich.

But the turning point was the humiliating 0-6 defeat at Nottingham

Forest in February 2003, which sent Stoke to the bottom of the league. "That result really knocked us sideways," says Tony of the Forest game. "That was one of the few times I rung Gunnar up, after that 6-0 defeat – because I don't like pestering people – and said to him, unless we get a few players in, you can write this off, because the players that everybody's telling me at the football club are good enough, they're *not* good enough by a country-mile. To be fair to him, he allowed me to get a few players in, and off we went. I'd listened to people's views within the football club for far far too long, and that was the point that I thought, No, he has to be told the truth, whether he likes it or not."

Tony & Kevan celebrate Akinbiyi's goal against Reading

The two key loan players Tony brought in were striker Ade "yes-him-again" Akinbiyi and goalkeeper Mark Crossley. Crossley was crucial; he didn't just make fine saves, he organised and galvanised the defence, on and off the pitch. There were seven clean-sheets in his 10 games, and it was this that rescued Stoke from the oblivion of relegation.

Of course, that season came down to the final game at home to promotion-seeking Reading (already in the play-offs), a game that turned out to be crucial to the future of Stoke City. The Potters just needed a point; if they lost, then rivals Brighton would need to win at bottom club Grimsby in order to send Stoke down instead.

Tony had no intentions of losing to Reading, whose away form of 12 wins he described as "triffic" (a word he used increasingly around this time). "They are a good counter-attacking side, so we've got to be careful we don't get caught with our pants down. But there's no way we can go out and play for a draw. This really is literally a cup final for our lads."

It was a tense first half at The Brit, but Stoke came out the brightest in the second half. This was just as well as Brighton took the lead in their game in the 47th minute. A single goal by Reading could send Stoke down.

Thankfully, on 55 minutes James O'Connor released Lewis Neal to cross to Akinbiyi, who lost his marker and coolly headed the ball home on the run. The crowd went crazy, more so when they heard Grimsby had equalised.

Take two bottles into the shower?...or something like that

With their 1-0 win on the final day, the 20,477 crowd celebrated in the sun, for once a Tony Pulis Barmy Army. With 15 players out of contract at the end of the season it was a big victory for the club, and a lot for Tony to mull over. "After we got annihilated 6-0 at Nottingham Forest on February 22nd everyone outside Stoke had us to not only go down but probably to finish at the very bottom. It's a very very big day for the future of this football club. I've always put the club and the team first. I'm desperate to be successful for them."

This was just as well, as Tony now wonders what would have happened to Stoke City if the club had gone down that season: "I think the Icelandic directors had had a rude awakening – running a football club in England wasn't a walk in the park that they thought it was going to be. I don't think they thought it was going to be as tough as they found it.

"If we'd had got relegated that year, I'm not so sure what they'd have done. It would have been a massive-massive blow to them financially, and I'm not sure if they would have walked away or kept it going for a year or two."

Somehow Tony Pulis got through the chaos of that first season, and on to better times. But many still remember that day he first joined, when he iconically told the Sentinel:

"It doesn't matter to me whether I am 2nd, 3rd or 10th choice. What matters is I want to come here, and this is what I call a proper football club. Others might say it's a difficult job and not a good career move, but I don't look at it like that at all. It's a fantastic job. I am proud to be the manager."

Part 2 - A New Era, But What To Call It?

Since that spirited end to the 2002/03 season, Stoke haven't really looked like being relegated again. In fact the only other periods in

Sent off against Millwall

Stoke's history that compare (length of time safe from relegation) are the celebrated Matthews era (1930s/40s) and the Waddington era (1960s/70s).

However, in 2003 there were still doubts as to what Tony Pulis could bring to the party. As a player, none of his sides had ever finished higher than 12th in Division 1 (now the Championship) or as a manager, 18th. Even John Rudge had finished 3rd (as a player) and 8th (as a manager).

With Rudge supporting him behind the scenes, Pulis started from first principles. Big burly defenders, a tight midfield, and balls being propelled into channels for tall strikers to head down...or occasionally head in. It wasn't pretty, but it was effective, steadying the Stoke ship whilst Pulis pushed and probed the market to find better exponents of his style.

So, after a promising start to the 2003/04 season – winning 3-0 at Derby and even briefly hitting the top of the league – they then got knocked out of the League Cup at home to Tony's former club Gillingham (0-2), and the club slid briefly down to a suicidal 22nd position (of 24).

But Tony was reshaping the team with several new signings, including Gifton Noel-Williams from Watford. By the time Stoke met Reading again just before Christmas, they were a different side. There were only four players remaining in Stoke's starting line-up that had begun the May game, including striker Ade "now-signed-permanently-*again*" Akinbiyi, and the gifted Dutch winger Peter Hoekstra, who'd somehow been persuaded to join The

Ade wins league player of the month!

Potters by John Rudge in 2001 from Ajax (yes, the one in Amsterdam). Despite Hoekstra's ankle operation, Tony was determined to have him as his reliable left-sided midfielder. Hoekstra returned his faith by taking a 50% pay cut to remain with Tony and the club.

It was no surprise that Tony was particularly desperate to fix his leaky defence. The team had shipped 12 goals in 6 games, including a hat-trick from former-Stokie Peter Thorne in a frustrating 2-3 home defeat by Cardiff. By December he'd already tried nearly a dozen different combinations at the back. But with a crucial new loan-signing, Stoke managed a 1-0 midweek victory at Alan Pardew's West Ham United, their first win at Upton Park in 30 years (with Tony again describing Stoke's performance as "triffic!").

The game marked the debut of defender Gerry Taggart from Micky Adams' Premier League Leicester side. For some reason Tony liked the look of Taggart: he was a tough-looking defender, he was out of favour at his club, and had even been sent off against Stoke the previous season. Perfect.

As he hadn't played for sometime, Tony rewarded his great performance achieving a clean-sheet at Upton Park with a diplomatic "few days off to recover". He wanted him fresh to take on Steve Coppell's

Reading, riding high in 5th place.

The Reading game in December 2003 was a particular watershed. A meagre 11,212 crowd saw a Hoekstra masterclass against a talented Reading side featuring Marcus Hahnemann, Nicky Shorey and Steve Sidwell. Hoekstra's hat-trick in the 3-0 win was blistering, particularly his

In a lonely place

25 yard goal-of-the-season strike.

To some this was the real statement of intent by a Tony Pulis side. With Hoekstra back to fitness and Taggart, who was soon signed full time, the side was finally finding a balance, winning five of their next six games, with even Noel-Williams and Akinbiyi finally putting some goals away. The club rose to mid-table, and haven't struggled at this level since. Was this the new...Pulis-era?

This was new territory for Tony, but there was always the problem of funding. The Icelandic board's response for new players was to impose two hopelessly inadequate Icelandic trialists on Tony, whom he would contemptuously refer to as Triggy and Ziggy. Then they called on him to play veteran Toddi Gudjonsson, who came on as a late sub at Coventry only to be out-paced and out-muscled by weary opponents who had already played nearly 90 gruelling minutes.

But despite all this, Tony's side was chasing the play-offs to the Premier League. Now Stoke were actually beating a lot of the top sides (for a change!) like Nottingham Forest (2-1), Sunderland (3-1), West Ham (1-0), and promoted West Brom (4-1).

And they nearly got revenge on Gillingham. In the last game of the season at the Britannia Stadium, Gillingham needed a point to stay up. Luckily for The Gills, the referee didn't see Carl Asaba's late header crossing the Gillingham goal-line, and the game ended 0-0. The following season, Stoke won 2-0, and Gillingham were relegated after failing to win their last game – Crewe won their game and stayed up.

Stoke finished a respectable 11th, Tony's then highest ever finish.

The Infamous Binary Season of 2004/05

There is a famous saying about Binary: "There are 10 types of people in the world: Those who understand binary, and those who don't."

Mystified? Well, so were Stoke fans.

Binary, for those who remember their old Maths lessons, is made up of "1"s and "0"s. And that's all that Stoke fans saw between 23rd October 2004 and 19th February 2005, as Stoke City's league results looked like a secret binary message made up of "1"s and "0"s. They were all 1-0, 0-1 or just 0-0.

The only exception to this was the first result, a luxurious 1-1 goal-fest with Leicester. Yes, TWO GOALS IN A SINGLE GAME!! Wow. Little did Stoke fans realise that wouldn't see more than a single goal for the next 17 games.

①①①⓪①⓪①①⓪⓪①①⓪①⓪①⓪①⓪⓪⓪①⓪①⓪①⓪①⓪①①⓪⓪

These are the results of that sequence of 18 games, looking not unlike a secret espionage code! [It is actually 61,612,889,434, not secret code but coincidently the total number of downloads made from the Apple App Store.] But what many don't remember was that there were in fact THIRTEEN other league games that season that also fitted the binary system, making 31 binary games in all.

Ironically, the season had started lively enough, with wins against the likes of Wolves, Derby and Cardiff. After 8 games Stoke actually topped the table (again) with a thrilling 10-man 3-2 victory over Ipswich at The Britannia Stadium watched by an enthralled crowd of over 23,000 (although admission prices had been slashed that day). The winner, of course, was scored by Ade "who-else?" Akinbiyi.

But Tony Pulis' major concern was how thin his squad was. "There was no investment at all into the football team at that time," he said, looking back on that season. "Our budget was a bottom-4 budget in the Championship, but we still managed to over-achieve in respect of budgets and money spent. But nobody talks about that, just the results. In my opinion we were over-achieving massively, but a lot of supporters didn't realise that."

In fact, Tony's only real signings were goalkeeper Steve Simonsen on a free and (gulp!) ex-Port Vale midfielder, Dave Brammer. Supporters expecting a push towards the Premiership were left bewildered.

The 120 days that shook the world...sort of...

After the Ipswich game, and the cold wind of winter approaching, Stoke battened down the hatches. Their prime concern was not to concede and therefore not to lose, and watching this spectacle became a pretty joyless experience for many.

The up-side was that after losing 0-2 at high-flying West Ham, Stoke wouldn't lose by conceded two goals for 5 months, which at the time was quite a novelty for them. In fact by Christmas, Stoke were in a comfortable 6th place after five 1-0 wins. This was binary at its purest.

Thanks for the memories, Ade, it's been good while it lasted

But after Christmas, the team then lost 5 games in a row by 0-1, the last one being at home to Leeds, striker Ade Akinbiyi's final game. Despite finding his confidence again under Tony Pulis, becoming Player Of The Year and being top-scorer, he fell out with the club over a promised contract, and held a sit-down protest in John Rudge's office, demanding to see the Chairman. After arriving on a free from Palace, Akinbiyi left Tony Pulis for the last time to join Steve Cotterill's Burnley for £600,000.

Fans took it badly, blaming Tony approach to football. "It just shows," complained one, "how bad things are, that Ade can leave for a team who aren't even any better than us." It also left Tony one striker short. Failing to bring in Bobby Zamora or Rob Hulse, Tony instead brought in loanee Kenwyne Jones, who immediately made a positive impression (mainly with his somersault goal-celebration).

But it wasn't just Akinbiyi who was frustrated over contract talks and team investment. Chairman Gislason was forced into clear-the-air talks with the first-team over their frustration with the club's regime. This included lack of funds available for new players and the uncertainty over the renewal of Tony Pulis' contract, which the players felt was unsettling the squad.

During this period, frustrated fans had to wait 584 minutes for a Stoke goal. But curiously enough, without Akinbiyi results picked up dramatically with 5 wins in 6 games, and six goals by Gifton Noel-Williams! Finally, the binary curse was lifted with another exciting 3-2 victory, this time against Leicester. But there was an unfortunate consequence.

The Very Last Thing You Want

On Thursday 3rd March, a tragedy beset the club that would have serious repercussions for Stoke City FC. During the day it began to filter through that Tony Pulis...had won...Manager Of The Month for February 2005, a month heavily scarred by the death-throes of the binary results sequence. Fans who wanted rid of Tony, bored of the unadventurous tactics, knew it would be even more difficult to unseat him. On the other hand, fans loyal to the manager knew the award was cursed, leading to an immediate downturn of results. As for the Icelandic board, it just added to their indecision over Tony's future.

Nobody can remember where they were when Tony Pulis won Manager Of The Month during the "Binary" season

As it was, Stoke continued their run with two 2-0 wins (Brighton and Sheffield United). It looked like the curse had finally been lifted. But after the tightness of the binary games, the floodgates opened at the other end too as (much to Tony's horror) Stoke conceded 8 goals in three straight defeats. In fact in their last 10 games, Stoke lost 7.

The net result was that they fell away from the play-off positions, finishing a disappointing 12th (of 24). Of course, Tony Pulis was more pragmatic about the season, observing that Stoke City had survived comfortably, whilst the less resilient Nottingham Forest, who had beaten Stoke 6-0 two seasons before, were relegated. And, for all the talk of Binary Results and negative football, average attendances at The Brit were the highest since Lou Macari's promotion season (despite no games against West Brom).

But what was more famously remembered about the 2004/05 season was that Tony's Stoke side only managed 36 goals – only Rotherham (bottom by a mile) scored less (35). Also, they conceded only 38 goals – only Wigan (promoted) conceded less (35). After looking through these fabulous statistics, the by now weary Icelandic board put the club up for sale. They felt they'd spent enough to be a Premier team by now (they hadn't), only they weren't there yet. Some of the board certainly felt that Tony had spent enough of their money.

Their next step was unclear. Rumour had it that the board thought that Peter Coates was poised to buy them out, and he favoured Tony, who thus got his new "rolling" contract. However, when Coates put in what they felt was a derisory offer, the board weren't impressed, and thus felt they didn't need Tony anymore. So they decided on one last roll of the dice, as long as it was with a more conducive manager.

Three months after being pronounced Manager Of The Month, Tony Pulis was out of a job again. Like Thordarson before him, Tony had been given nearly 3 seasons by the Icelandic board to deliver, before they ran out of patience. Some, including Coates, felt he had been treated shabbily. Years later, Tony would look back on this moment with some bitterness: "The lowest point of my time at Stoke was knowing before I got the sack that I was going to get the sack!"

On 28th June 2005, Stoke chairman Gunnar Gislason famously announced: "The reason for this change is that, despite all the good work he has done, he has failed to implement the strategy of exploiting foreign markets for players, and it is felt we will again fail to exploit those markets this summer with him in control."

Many Stoke fans who had endured a gruelling season, weren't too unhappy to see Tony sacked, although the "failing to exploit the foreign transfer market" reason given by the Icelandic board was a curiosity. The press had a field day with that one.

It hadn't gone unnoticed that Tony had cleared out most of Thordarson's Icelandic players, and wasn't too keen on hiring anymore without proven pedigree. When Tony was painstakingly negotiating his new contract, there had been a healthy exchange of views on bringing in unknown, cheap, but potentially lucrative foreign players. But there was a risk that they could turn out to be useless for English football, and without stats or the ability to watch them play, just as many duffers would turn up.

Subsequently, Tony seemed less inclined to search abroad for players, particularly as he had his own UK contact network. In the end, both sides had to settle for a draw, but more Icelandic players arrived all the same. As Tony observed: "I have been very pro-British players all through my career. I would rather deal with players I know, players I can find out about. But I recognise it is a different level now."

Although many of his teams were fairly cosmopolitan, it was fair to say (particularly with his later squads) that most of the players he brought in had already been tried and blooded by other UK clubs. An example of this was Malian striker Mamady Sidibe, who'd already played for Swansea and Gillingham. Tony signed Mama in June 2005...only for him to be sacked 4 days later.

As more and more foreign managers and players flooded into the English game, it looked like the once young gun from South Wales might be out of touch with the changing trends. Only six years before he'd been part of "a new generation of up-and-coming managers". The future for Tony Pulis did not look so good on paper. Maybe this would be the end of the road?

He was particularly hampered by the Binary Season of 2004/05. Whether he liked it or not, it had effectively crystallised the public image of Tony Pulis' playing style (or

Tony leaves after being sacked

"Pulisball" as sceptical Stoke fans referred to it) for the whole world to see. Despite all he has achieved as a manager, that season is the reference point that fans and media use – even today – when judging him.

What still bewilders people is how Tony managed to win the Coca-Cola-sponsored Manager Of The Month during the Binary Season, a fact so bizarre it appears to have been air-brushed from history. Well, although Stoke had won 1-0 at soon-to-be-promoted Wigan (with that first goal in 584 minutes), Tony still had to pip the award ahead of Mick McCarthy, who had just taken Sunderland to the top of the league, and Alan Pardew, with promotion pushing West Ham. What may have tipped it in Tony's favour was the fact that the Coca-Cola Awards panel was headed by a certain Coca-Cola Ambassador, none-other-than Sky Sports pundit and former Stoke-man Chris Kamara.

This may go some way to explain why most people found the whole thing "Unbelievable".

Chapter 4 – **Plymouth, Plymouth, Plymouth! (2005/06)**

Part 1 – Er, Boston United

Travelling didn't seem to bother Tony Pulis anymore. He'd obviously got used to it.

Stoke fans had been perplexed to find that whilst working in The Potteries, he still lived in Bournemouth, five hours drive away. But Tony was philosophical about this: "It's a big help on Saturday night when I'm driving home alone with no one to disturb me. It gives me the peace and quiet I need to run the game through my head in great detail. It also means that when I'm up here in Stoke there are no distractions from home. I'm not the best person to be around after we've lost!"

What was there not to fear?

That said, the logic was that after being turfed out of Stoke City, he would return to football somewhere in the south, with perhaps the likes of Brighton, Reading, Swindon or Bristol Rovers. As he'd managed both Bournemouth and Portsmouth, the Southampton job, which he'd been offered years before, now seemed logically out of the question (more unforgiving supporters). But then again that hadn't stopped Harry Redknapp who had somehow managed all three, although he'd just got The Saints relegated in 2005 and was slowly making his way to the door. Maybe Tony would succeed Harry again in managing a south coast club? Stranger things have happened.

And stranger things did happen. Instead of heading south, Tony suddenly popped up in the north at League 2 side Boston United helping out his old friend, the controversial Steve Evans (now with newly promoted Rotherham). Up near Skegness with his family, Tony agreed to cast his eye over Boston in September 2005 after "The Pilgrims" had started their 4th season in The Football League with an 8 game win-less sequence.

As the club searched for a new full-time coach, (and Steve Evans searched for a solicitor as he was being charged with tax fraud at the time) Tony joined training sessions, helping them to explore different avenues in their style of play. The players responded well, immediately winning their first game of the season, 3-2 against top-side Rochdale, and then drawing at Bury.

Pilgrim Alan White, who netted the winner in the Rochdale game, was full of praise for Tony: "He's organised and gets things in your head about doing it simply. Straight away the lads were buzzing. He's a brilliant coach and came up with a lot of good things, good information for us – particularly with the 3-4-3 formation we played on Saturday – and helped us out."

There was even idle talk of Tony succeeding Evans, although the latter obviously didn't think much of the idea: "I am delighted to have him around, even though it is only very short-term. He is a top class manager with a huge knowledge of the game and I have no doubt that he will be back managing in the Championship sooner rather than later." ie. Go away!

The Pilgrim's Progress

Meanwhile, another club also nicknamed "The Pilgrims" were in need of his services as they struggled in the lower reaches of The Championship. Plymouth Argyle had got themselves promoted in 2004, but had struggled ever since. At the start of the 2005/06 season they had lost 5 league games in a row, and nestled in 23rd (of 24) position.

As Tony lived just along the coast, had Championship experience, had never been relegated, and would bring a bit of discipline to the place, he certainly seemed like a good fit. But he had a blunt message for the directors about the team: "Not good enough to stay up," he told them, although it wasn't anything they hadn't already heard from their own supporters.

The Plymouth chairman obviously concurred: "We believe we've got a man who will work with us; be serious about his job; will wheel and deal; will work within budgets; will help us with budgets; will not give money away freely, will treat it like his own; and will make us a force again." It was nice for Tony to have a chairman who so believed in him.

"He is on a 12-month rolling contract, which suits both parties and we hope it is for a long time.

"He has got a steely determination about him; I don't think he suffers fools gladly; he had a reputation, perhaps, for falling out with people, but I think he's mellowed a bit; and he's got a certain charm about him."

The Charmed One

The "charmed" one saw his immediate challenge as similar to when he first became Portsmouth or Stoke manager: survival and consolidation.

"Anyone know this guy? I can't seem to shake him off!" The Pulis/Kemp dream team

"It's a big challenge, a big club, massive potential. But to suggest that we should be competing for a Premiership slot [in the short term] is non-sensical. The likes of Southampton, Sheffield United, Wolves, Leeds, Norwich, Crystal Palace and many others have wage budgets on a different planet to ours. There are managers who are spending millions and millions of pounds that we are going to have to compete against. I've never had that luxury in my life, I've always been in a position where I've been fire-fighting."

When asked about his reputation and being pigeon-holed, Tony rebuffed: "I like my teams to be competitive. Supporters pay good money to see their team compete. If we've got the players in the team to pass the ball, we will pass the ball. But the players have got to understand that the work-ethic has to be second to none. If we are going to punch above our weight, they have got to be fit; they have got to be prepared; they have got to be committed.

"Sometimes, because you are so desperate to win, so desperate to put a performance in for your supporters, people may put you into the category of being aggressive. But I've built teams over my career and those teams have been decent sides, decent footballing sides."

He'd also become a tad philosophical: "I'm not a great fellow for going on the telly, spouting my mouth off, and attempting to build an image up that I can then con someone else with. I'm not a glossy manager. I'm not one of those pretty books in a bookshop that everyone picks up and, when you open it up, there's no substance inside. I think I'm probably that dusty one at the back that, when you pick it up and start reading it, you really enjoy it."

But there was another factor that made it a dream-team for Plymouth, and that was Tony's long-suffering side-kick David Kemp.

"Kempy" had been a prolific goal scorer in his day. He'd started with 10 goals in 35 games for Crystal Palace under the flamboyant Malcolm Allison. Then, when Terry Venables came in, he was sold to Portsmouth in 1976 where he scored 30 goals in 64 games. But he then became a bit of a Plymouth hero after signing for them in 1979, and playing alongside a young Gary Megson. Despite injuries and

Kempy practicing his Irish jig

ever-changing sides, he managed an impressive 44 goals in 91 games, celebrating his many goals with a familiar clenched-fist salute...and the occasional Irish jig!

Later David Kemp returned as Plymouth's manager in early 1990, helping them stay in Division 2 (now The Championship). Curiously, in his only full season in charge (1990/91), Argyle had a solid home record (only losing 3), but a grim away record (only winning 2). However, fans and media suspected that the years Kemp had spent coaching the long-ball specialists Wimbledon in their crazy-gang 1980s heyday had rubbed off on him a bit too much. Attendances dropped by nearly a quarter, and Kemp, who fiercely denied his tactics were strictly long-ball, began to refuse interviews. During the following season, the club was taken over and Kemp was replaced by the arguably more glamorous former-England star Peter Shilton. Several weeks later, poor results had sent them down.

"I kept them up for two years on a shoestring budget," he later growled, "and since I left they have spent a lot of money and been relegated."

So, in September 2005, Plymouth fans, board-members and local media were under no illusions as to what the new dream-team were offering: Survival. It may not be pretty, but it would be survival.

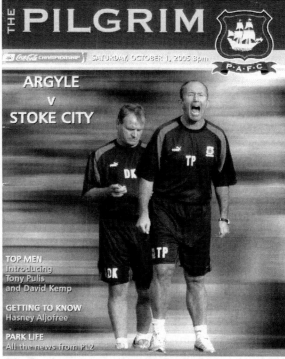

Ironically they were appointed a few days after a 1-0 win against Steve Cotterill's Burnley, putting in a gritty physical performance (much to the annoyance of Cotterill) almost as if to impress the new bosses. It took the team briefly up to 20th (of 24).

The first home game...it just had to be against Stoke City
(Reproduced courtesy of Plymouth Argyle FC)

Instead of waiting for the two week break in fixtures (due to a World Cup qualifier) that was 3 games down the line, Tony and Kempy jumped straight in. Tony reasoned: "I still had a year of my contract with Stoke to run, so it was quite easy for me to sit at home and take the money, but I really wanted to step up and be involved. I want to be in there, I want to smell the dressing-room, and see what we have got in there and what we haven't got."

What the smell obviously told him was that they were facing a tough set of fixtures.

Tony's first game in charge was away at just-relegate-from-Premier Southampton, where Harry Redknapp was still hogging the top-job (though not for much longer). The new Plymouth regime ground out a commendable 0-0 draw despite Harry trying to catch them out by bringing on as sub a speedy new young player called Theo Walcott. Tony responded by substituting Bjarni Gudjonsson in the second half...just as he had done in his very first game as Stoke's manager.

Next up was away at top-of-the-table Sheffield United, who made it 10 wins in 11 games by beating Argyle 2-0; comfortable enough for manager Neil Warnock to bring on a certain Vincent Pericard as a sub. Could it get anymore difficult?

As if ordained by the gods, Tony's first home game in charge of Plymouth was against none other than his previous club Stoke City.

Part 2 - Meanwhile, Back At The Farm

The Potters had duly hired a proper foreign manager – not just a Welsh one this time. But for the Icelandic Consortium, it really was a case of jumping out of the frying pan and into the fire. Johan Boskamp wasn't just a loose cannon, his antics made him seem...truly surreal.

Like Tony, Boskamp also asked about the lively atmosphere at the Meet-the-Manager evening. He then went in and told them: "John Rudge told me you come to

Tony in full flow at Argyle

hang me from the lamppost, but I think he was only joking." It seems Rudge wound up all the managers that way.

However, Boskamp soon fell out with John Rudge, refusing to work with him or the assistant manager over a misunderstanding in a November 2-1 win at Coventry. This was despite Rudge talking Boskamp out of resigning early on. Results and form were subsequently all over the place, best illustrated by their 2005/06 goal difference of 54-63 – Tony's 2004/05 miserly goal-difference had been 36-38.

Boskamp interviews and press conferences were often just plain weird. He famously answered "I am not a man!" when asked to reveal a secret about himself; "I'm really a woman." But then he also denied that he was a dictator: "I'm not Adolf Hitler", which was fair enough.

But at least he took the foreign market more seriously, and as his reward he was given serious money to exploit it, which was more than his predecessor had been offered. He thus broke the club's record transfer fee by signing Guinea international Sammy Bangoura for £900,000. However, Bangoura went missing after playing for Guinea, before finally turning up, arrested for trying to bring another African into the country. Stoke were soon to discover that "exploiting the foreign markets" did have certain unforeseen side-affects.

So it was not lost on the media that Plymouth's 77th minute winner in a 2-1 victory over Stoke (coming back from 0-1 down) was scored by a Hungarian international, brought on to replace an Icelander (Gudjonsson), with an assist by a Frenchman. City twice hit the post, but Argyle hung on for Tony's first win, which the media naturally portrayed as Tony's Revenge.

After Tony had faced *his* old club, Plymouth hero Paul Sturrock returned with his Sheffield Wednesday side for a tough 1-1 draw. Sturrock had left Argyle for Premier League Southampton, although he was soon dumped (after only 13 games) making way for Harry Redknapp.

Just as tough was a visit to Ian Holloway's QPR, which brought in another point (1-1). A few weeks later, Plymouth beat them 3-1 in the return game, and as a result Holloway was soon sent on gardening leave. He too would soon be moving south.

But Tony became immediately aware of how much work was needed at Plymouth. Apart from a general air of despondency that hung around the club when he arrived, he was alarmed at the player's poor fitness levels. In particular he observed amongst them the recently-signed Nigerian Taribo West, him of bewildering Mohican-dreadlock haircuts and a shadowy background. Although he'd given his age as 32, it was later revealed that he was 44! Taribo was discreetly moved on.

Also soon on his way again was Bjarni Gudjonsson, whom Tony had already sold once after inheriting him at Stoke. In the January 2006 transfer window, his contract was cancelled, despite having 6 months left on it. Tony said Gudjonsson's style of play "did not suit the team". "It didn't at Stoke and it hasn't here. That's nothing against him. There's no personal vendetta or grudge. Bjarni has been smashing, he's a good kid. I have no problems with Bjarni." But you couldn't help but feel sorry for the guy.

Results slowly improved around Christmas/January, gaining 5 wins and 2 draws in 8 games, with Tony's loan signings stiffening Plymouth's resistance. In a 2-0 win against promotion-seeking Crystal Palace, Nick Chadwick scored after only 12 seconds, the fastest Argyle goal in history. With the team moving away from relegation, one of Tony's loanees caught people's attention more than most.

Portsmouth Striker Vincent Pericard had been brought to the UK by Harry Redknapp. Touted around as "ex-Juventus", he'd in fact

Waiting for Vincent Pericard to score

only made only one appearance as substitute for the Italian super-club. But it was so believed that he had potential that a documentary was supposedly made about him called 'The Man Who'll Be Worth Billions'. After a decent start for Pompey, he'd suffered several injuries, and was taking loan moves to get his fitness back.

Although Pericard was only 6ft 1in (small by Pulis-standards), Tony reckoned he could do a job for him, and gave him his first start at (of all places) The Britannia Stadium in the 0-0 draw with Stoke on Valentine's Day. Tony was given a perhaps surprisingly warm welcome by Potters fans, and equally generous were his strikers who missed two open goals. "It was a fantastic reception. I'm very, very pleased," Tony said after the game. He then let his guard down slightly by adding: "You sometimes worry about what people might think of your time here. The welcome was very much appreciated. Unfortunately, it wasn't a fantastic match!"

But then four days later it did not go unnoticed that Pericard scored a hat-trick for Plymouth on his home debut. Surely he would now fulfil his potential?

The Stone-Banker

Plymouth continued to hold their ground, even with top sides like Wolves (2-0), away at Preston (0-0) and a 0-0 game that they should have won at rampant Leeds United, where they were denied a late penalty, which Tony was casually philosophical about: "A definite penalty, 2 yards inside the box. I'm 120% biased, so I see everything through green eyes, but I think it was a stone-banker penalty."

Stone-banker or not, Plymouth signed off the season with an emotional 2-1 win against Ipswich, with long-serving local lad Mickey Evans bringing the house down by obligingly scoring the winner in his fairy-tale last game for the club. Pilgrim fans went home that day with big smiles on their faces.

Argyle had finished safely in 14th place with 56 points. Although one place and two points behind Stoke, Tony had the satisfaction that despite them changing managers and scoring a lot more goals, The Potters had finished one place lower than Tony's binary effort the previous season.

Tony's mission had been accomplished comfortably with a number of spirited performances for fans to mull over. The way ahead looked steady, establishing Plymouth as a mid-table Championship side pushing for a play-off spot for the Premier League. But some of the Pulis-Kemp tactics deployed to secure safety, gave Plymouth fans an axe to grind.

Tony setting a safety target of 53 points in February had hardly endeared him to over-ambitious fans, who suddenly had acquired delusions of making the play-offs! Attendances were down on average by 2,500 to 13,776, although in fairness they continued to fall in subsequent seasons under other less-austere managers. "We have got to make this place a fortress," he'd said of the Home Park support, an ambition he sought for all his clubs. In contrast, it was felt that he had parked-the-bus too often away from home, where his players had amassed only 13 goals in 23 games (one less than his previous "binary" season).

But there was little doubt in people's minds that the following season would be better. But for whom?

Chapter 5 – The Return Of The King (2006-08)

Part 1 – The Men Least Likely

They say you should never go back, it's always a disappointment.

Mourinho, Keegan, Dalglish and even Matt Busby had tried it to little success.

However, for Tony Pulis, going-back seemed to be a career strategy.

He returned to Bristol Rovers where he became youth coach whilst playing alongside Alan Ball, Mick Channon and Ian Holloway. He returned to Bournemouth where he became first team coach and ultimately the manager. He returned to Gillingham to taste his first managerial success with promotion and a trip to Wembley. Even going home to Newport culminated in a historic meeting with Harry Redknapp.

But returning to Stoke did NOT seem like a winning idea.

Neither did it seem like a winning idea for Peter Coates to return to the helm at Stoke City. Coates, with his stadia catering business and warring directors, had been chairman through some turbulent years, overseeing the club sinking into the Third Division and drifting through a stack of managers. There had been flashes of success, such as the Wembley Autoglass win and eventual promotion out of the Third, but Coates saw little in the way of praise. Fans had little time for him, believing him to be unambitious and penny-pinching. So when the proposed

Tony returns! It was like he'd never been away...

move from The Victoria Ground to The Britannia Stadium was announced, he was further demonised with protests from the terraces, resulting in him standing down as chairman.

After the club sank into the third tier again, Coates and his colleagues tried unsuccessfully to recruit Tony. But a few months later it didn't matter, as an Icelandic Consortium bought up 66% of Stoke's shares for £3.5m. Coates remained a minority shareholder, but his presence at the club was not always appreciated by the new owners, particularly when Coates' stock grew and theirs declined.

Despite the Icelanders' best intentions, the club was still a shambles in 2002 – a suitable example being the farcical circumstances behind the original hiring of Tony as manager. With the Icelandic directors not

always around, it was understandable that Tony and Peter Coates would forge a close footballing friendship.

For Coates, things were falling into place. His modest set of betting shops had led his daughter Denise to help him launch the internet betting sensation bet365. He was soon on his way to being one of the richest men in football.

A signed photo of Tony signing a photo...

With the Icelandic Consortium keen to sell Stoke City in 2005/06, Coates initially tried to set up a consortium of his own, although he claimed he couldn't find any local businessmen who'd work with him! ...or at least stump up the necessary cash. Eventually, Coates finally struck a deal to buy the club back himself (costing him about £5m). However, Denise Coates later revealed: "If Tony Pulis hadn't been willing to come back, dad would not have wanted to do it. It's one thing having the resources, it's quite another having the faith in a manager to achieve success with those resources."

Although his family were sceptical about him coming back, Peter Coates was adamant, particularly about Tony for whom he always had a "great deal of confidence": "I thought he hadn't been given anything like enough credit for what he did when he was in control under the Icelanders. I think there's certain ingredients you need as a manager. He's a good judge of a player, his teams are well prepared and well organised, and he gets the best out of his players. I don't know what more you can do as a manager."

When Coates eventually contacted him, it put Tony in an awkward position. He had done the ground work to start building at Plymouth, but to have someone phone him and show such faith in him was an extraordinary moment in his life: "I had no qualms about coming back. Peter rang me and said he was going to buy the club, but only if I came back as well. Yes, it was an enormous pressure on me, but he thought Stoke City could be an established Premier League club."

The media would be shocked, but it was the Stoke supporters whom they would have to win over. To the fans the Coates-Pulis pairing wouldn't exactly be a dream-team, it would be more like the ultimate nightmare!

"Peter said: 'I'm tough enough to take it on, are you tough enough?' It was difficult for me to say 'No, I don't fancy it, Peter; all the best!'"

However, it was the writer David Johnson who put it best when describing their pluck on this momentous occasion: "Balls the size of Wales, the pair of them."

Running Down The Pilgrims

Plymouth were suitably aghast. What did Stoke, who'd only finished one place above them, have to offer that they didn't? At first the board resisted the approach for their manager, but soon realised it was futile.

However much Tony tried not to be disparaging to Plymouth, by talking about the major potential for Stoke, it only made it sound like he was running down The Pilgrims. Despite all his good work, he was vilified by Plymouth fans for dumping them in this manner. In June 2006 it was unclear whether he had any fans behind him at all, on either side of the fence.

Initially the more solvent Peter Coates didn't flash his cash around much, whilst Tony immediately began to struggle to attract the players he needed in the August transfer window. So, as the season started, the sole signing of the supposedly-ex-Juventus-striker Vincent Pericard on a free transfer hardly impressed the sceptical Stoke fans. This was NOT what they had been promised. In fairness, Coates spent more time and effort steadying the ship financially behind the scenes, in preparation for buying back the stadium and improving training facilities – the sorts of things that fans find so unsexy.

The opening day 0-1 defeat at newly promoted Southend was a grim start, but it was quickly forgotten after a stirring 2-0 defeat of Derby. It was followed by a string of poor results, including a truly dreadful defeat in the Carling Cup First Round.

How dreadful? Well, Stoke were dumped out of the Cup by 4th tier Darlington by 1-2...at home...with The Quakers down to 10 men after only

12 minutes...and Stoke fielding a strong side and taking the initial lead. "I apologise to the 3,600 who turned up to watch it," Tony said after this spectacle, no doubt relieved that more didn't bother turning up – those that did gave him a right earful. "Not only have we got beat, we have got beat by 10 men." It was doubly humiliating as Tony decided to give his son Anthony his first team debut in this game. Anthony would go on to make one substitute appearance for Stoke, before going on loan, to clubs

Stoke fans were understandably pleased to see Tony Pulis again...

such as Torquay, Plymouth, Grimsby, Bristol Rovers, Lincoln, Barnet and Stockport (where he scored his only first team goal). [Always under his father's shadow in the UK, Anthony Pulis would go on to find success with Orlando City, Stoke's affiliated side in the USA.]

The strike-partnership of Pericard and Mama Sidibe that didn't look quite right on paper, also didn't look quite right on grass. In fairness, Pericard did manage a goal, although it was against Darlington, a club struggling two leagues below Stoke; he only managed 2 more for the whole season.

The following week Stoke played host to Plymouth, now managed by – of all people – Ian Holloway, who at least acknowledged that Tony had left him a decent set of lads. But even "Ollie" noticed the strange atmosphere at The Brit, where vengeful away supporters were joined by dissatisfied home supporters in barracking Tony in a tense 1-1 draw. It was still only August.

At the next home game against Burnley, Stoke went 0-1 down in the first minute, and never looked like getting back in the game. They didn't. The Stoke crowd were ready to turn on their manager, but it was nothing that Tony wasn't expecting from Potters fans: "They tell you what they think, but I'm one of those who would rather that than sneak round the corner and not tell you what they think."

The whole new Pulis-Coates team looked on the verge of calamity before it had even got started, with Stoke starting the season with only one win in 11 games. Tony had actually managed to sign two key players before the window closed, but even with them the side wasn't gelling.

Less than a dozen games in, and the fans smelt blood. Disaffected supporters were planning a red card protest against Tony. Ten thousand 6"x4" red cards were printed with "Give Pulis His Cards" on one side and "Time To Get Rolling Tone" on the other. A group calling themselves "The 1972 Committee" claimed that "It is a peaceful protest and not one aimed at the players. We simply want to put pressure on Peter Coates to change the manager. We were opposed to Tony Pulis coming back, but were prepared to give him a chance. Not any more though."

Stoke fans were understa- ...etc

Coates responded by saying, "It would be crazy to change the manager so early in the season. I believe we have a good manager and he has my support. The guy hasn't been in the job five minutes. Give him a chance!"

The cards were due to be handed out to supporters before the home game with Preston, and could have thrown Stoke's season into civil war. Tony needed to act fast, and act decisively.

So he decided to phone-a-friend.

The Man Who Can Read Minds

Tony Pulis wasn't prepared to be rushed into buying. He wanted to build carefully. For once he had the opportunity to pick and choose a better class of players, ones that fitted his style, ones that had the right attitude. The two most notable features of this attitude were firstly their willingness to track-back and defend, without complaint and from whatever position they played, requiring them to be extra fit; and secondly to behave with discipline when it came to fouls, injuries and dealing with officials – no rolling around on the floor, no remonstrating with the referee. Earlier in his managerial career, his less-disciplined players had attracted a raft of unnecessary suspensions, something Tony was now in a position to be intolerant of.

One side-effect of this approach was his often infuriating habit of fielding players out of their normal position, in his belief that the team benefitted as a whole when all 11 players had the right attitude, his attitude.

One who didn't have this attitude was Sammy Bangoura. After driving Boskamp mad the previous season ("He has totally no respect for anyone! If I was a player (not a manager), I would kick him in his b***s!" exclaimed Johan, calmly), he turned up a month late for pre-season training. With Tony Pulis in charge, he might as well have not bothered turning up at all. His only start was the Burnley defeat – he lasted only 43 minutes before pulling up. He managed 50 more minutes of football at Stoke (as a substitute) before being moved on.

Others who were causing disharmony in the dressing room were also on their way within a few months. His actions were met with approval by the likes of Mama Sidibe, who was particularly glad to see the troublemakers go and for Tony to return: "He cleaned up the dressing room just as he promised he would. He is excellent at dealing with people – it sometimes feels as though he can read your thoughts."

As part of his Autumn dressing-room clean-up, Tony made two crucial signings from George Burley's Southampton: gifted defender Danny Higginbotham (£225,000) and iconic striker Ricardo Fuller (£500,000), both with the standard copper-bottomed Redknapp-approval (although H was now back at Portsmouth). They were joined by right-back Andy Griffin (returning to his first club) and Salif Diao (from Liverpool), a quality midfielder not known for trespassing in the opponent's half.

But to kick-start it all, there was a vital piece missing.

So he phoned up an old friend from his Bristol Rovers days, former-midfielder Paul Hendrie, about his son Lee. Lee Hendrie was a revered Aston Villa player and England international. "I was desperate to get some games under my belt after coming back from a calf injury but not getting much of a chance at first team level with Villa."

The chances of Tony getting Lee were slim. He had already been approached by Crystal Palace and QPR, and Lee knew and had worked with both of their managers (Peter Taylor and John Gregory). But Tony was persistent. "My dad told me he'd had a call from Stoke and that Tony Pulis would love me to go there. He said what a good bloke Tony was and reckoned that going on loan there would be my best option. I spoke to the manager on a Thursday by telephone then went in to see him the next morning, and although I wasn't a hundred per cent match fit he said 'I want you to play on Saturday'. That's what I wanted to hear. I was given a free role to set play up from midfield and get forward to score goals, and when the manager stressed that he wanted me to go out and enjoy my football that made up my mind. I was very nervous before my first match - it was the first time I'd ever played for anyone but Villa, and it was weird pulling on a different club's shirt. Things clicked straight away though."

Tony's inspired move to sign Villa's quality midfielder on loan just 24 hours before the crucial Preston game (the one earmarked for the Red-Card protest) was a real coup, capturing the imagination of the media and the fans.

When news filtered out about Hendrie's signing, there was an outcry of support from fans urging protestors to give Tony a chance. Amazingly, at the last minute the protestors agreed to postpone until a later date, admitting that Hendrie's signing was "the most exciting thing to have happened at City under Pulis". But they insisted it was just a postponement. Afterall, 10,000 red-cards to protest against Tony Pulis? They'd surely be needed some day.

In an exciting game against 3rd place Preston, Stoke (who had by now sunk to 21st place) had to settle for a 1-1 draw. But the great performance that day turned things around, and was spearheaded by Lee Hendrie, who could've scored a hat-trick, and the new Fuller-Sidibe striking partnership who managed one between them.

After the game, Tony had a spring back in his step: "I thought the supporters were fantastic. I thought we played some smashing football, but we should have scored more goals. I know what's wrong and what's needed." When asked about his critics in the crowd, he quipped: "The only supporter I worry about is the chairman!"

Tony had turned the corner...despite Ricardo already driving him round the bend.

The Road To Kingdom Come

Not only did Hendrie's presence capture the imagination and produce great performances, but it also brought immediate results, including a 4-0 win at Leeds in the very next game, then a 5-0 win against Norwich, and a 3-0 win against top-of-the-table Cardiff. By Christmas Stoke were 4th.

With further loan additions of Liam Lawrence and Rory Delap, Stoke were chasing a playoff position. Both Lawrence and Delap were soon signed permanently; part of what became a seemingly continuous flow of players from Sunderland. Although Delap broke his leg in only his second game for Stoke (ironically against Sunderland), Tony stood by him, signing him permanently 3 months later. This was even before he was aware of Delap's long-throw capabilities.

Tony still waiting to win over the fans

A formidable squad was beginning to take shape. Fans began to wake up to the fact that something was happening, although many still doubted whether Pulis was the man for the job. This was despite the fact that it was the new Pulis-men who were not just putting on the performances, but they were also getting the goals, particularly Fuller, Lawrence, Sidibe and Higginbotham. This was the new backbone for the team.

Of these four, the star that was emerging was striker Ricardo Fuller, whom Tony rated as one of his best signings, although he did little for his receding hairline. "Ric was a great signing, particularly for the price we paid. He's the reason I've got no hair, but he's an absolutely fantastic player!" Fuller could be astonishing to the point of breathtaking, like in the 3-1 win at West Brom in April 2007, where he volleyed the first and set up the other two goals. Despite only starting 26 games, he was top scorer, rewarded by his striking partner, Sidibe, acting as target man. But there was another side to Ricardo. He somehow got himself sent off twice and booked 9 times (usually for doing something unnecessarily daft), and he had the dodgiest knees in the Championship – the knees alone had failed medicals up and down the country before Stoke signed him. He also believed he could drive a car in the UK on a Jamaican licence – sadly he couldn't. It showed an emerging maturity in Tony, as he somehow just managed to tolerate it all.

For his first season back, Tony had done enough to show that he meant business. Naturally enough Tony won Manager Of The Month in April 2007, and naturally enough the season began to fizzle out as a result. Two late equalisers in consecutive games (Cardiff and Hull, both 1-1) effectively put paid to a play-off spot, and a final day 1-1 draw at QPR was never going to be enough. But the sound-bite was simple: it was Stoke's highest finish for over a decade (8th).

Part 2 – I Never Thought It Would Happen

The 2007/08 season was always going to be difficult for football manager Tony Pulis, even the day-to-day stuff. In later interviews he would quaintly refer to the process of dealing with his squad as "babysitting". This could have been a mellowing process on his part (yeah, right) or just a reaction to the fragility of 21st century footballers. Either way, with the Premier League close enough to touch, it certainly required a modified approach to his fire-brand manner of the past. He needed to be prepared for whatever life would throw at him.

Firstly, there was striker Vincent Pericard, slowly working his way down the pecking order as Stoke fans realised he wasn't as "ex-Juventus" as was first believed. In August 2007 he was sentenced to 4 months in prison for perverting the course of justice over who was driving his Mercedes at 103mph near Plymouth. He claimed it was his stepfather, the one that was in France at the time.

Tony's language was noticeably fatherly: "We can't condone what he has done but he is not a nasty or bad person. He has been very naive and made a mistake, which we have all done at some point."

Pericard only served one month in jail. Unfortunately, his electronic tag 'came off' soon after his release, and he was back inside.

As if that wasn't bad enough, then Tony had to deal with striker Mama Sidibe returning to the Britannia Stadium from international duty in October 2007 with a lot less blood than when he'd left. After his Mali side had beaten Togo to get to the Africa Cup, there had been rioting, and whilst running off the pitch Sidibe had received a nasty blow to the head, which was bleeding badly. But to compound that, as the team was holed up in the stadium tunnel, with an angry mob trying to get in to attack them, Sidibe had frustratedly put his fist through a window, severing a vein. There was blood everywhere, and people really were panicking now.

Tony celebrates the return of the fans

With his teammates trying to stop the bleeding and ambulances being turned back by the rioters, it was a miracle Sidibe survived. On the plus side, he hadn't been stabbed or shot as some reports had said; and amazingly he only missed 5 games, although Stoke lost 3 of them.

It probably explains why Stoke fans were more than patient with his progress that season, particularly as after playing 23 games, the striker still hadn't scored. Even Pericard had got off the mark. So Sidibe went to see the manager. Tony just smiled and said that goals were not his job that season, and that playing his position properly was more important. "Let me do the worrying," Tony told him, "and you just keep doing what I tell you to do." When Sidibe finally did score in his 24th game – what turned out to be the winner against Southampton in a 3-2 victory – the home crowd went crazy. How could they not do?

Then there was the bizarre story of goalkeeper Russell Hoult. Tony had signed him once already when he'd managed Portsmouth, but when Tony left, Hoult was soon sold to West Brom for a sizable profit. This time Tony picked him up from Albion for free in early 2007, mainly as The Baggies had dropped him like a stone after a raunchy video of him had been posted on the internet. It was hard to tell whether the Albion were more upset by the sex, the posting on the internet or the fact that

Hoult was allegedly wearing a club polo shirt in the vid.

For Tony it was just an opportunity to get a decent player whom other clubs might not have touched. As such he began to get a reputation for signing a few waifs and strays, giving them a chance to redeem themselves. It was good business; if the player responded, then it was a cheap signing of a good player that unfashionable Stoke might not have normally attracted; if the player became trouble, they could be moved on fairly easily.

In the case of Hoult, he heroically kept the bench warm for 14 months understudying Steve Simonsen. Before his arrival Tony didn't even keep a goalkeeper on the bench! Hoult actually made only two appearances for Stoke – in a penalty-shoot-out defeat against Rochdale after a 2-2 draw (in fairness he did save one of the penalties), and a 2-2 draw with Plymouth...where he was sent off.

Tony's Gang

Thankfully Tony didn't have to deal with all these shenanigans on his own. Over the years he had developed a "gang" around him to help him organise and supervise all the coaching and scouting.

Firstly there was David Kemp, who had been with Tony as coach and assistant manager at Portsmouth, Stoke, Plymouth, and then back at Stoke again. Kempy had actually been hired by Pompey as first team coach a few weeks before Tony arrived in January 2000. Since then they've worked so well together that they have been almost inseparable.

There was also Lindsay Parsons, whose coaching and scouting skills had followed Tony from Bristol Rovers to Gillingham, Bristol City, Portsmouth, Stoke, Plymouth and Stoke again. When at Rovers they actually only ever played 4 games together in the first team, conceding 8 goals. As they were both defenders, they were obviously not seen as a compatible partnership.

Not far behind was Mark O'Connor, who'd played with Tony at several clubs, before coaching with him at Gillingham, Portsmouth, Plymouth and Stoke. Mark was part of the 1987 AFC Bournemouth promotion team, scoring 7 from midfield. Tony was the only regular outfielder not to score that season.

Then there was Adrian Pennock, who'd played for Tony at Bournemouth and Gillingham, and had joined as a coach at Stoke in 2007.

Of course, Tony could always rely on the support of Stoke's Director Of Football, John Rudge, despite Tony continually teasing him about

TONY'S GANG!

"KEMPY"
(Dave Kemp)

Palace 1976 Player
+ Plymth Portsmouth/
Gillingham Player.
Wimbledon coach '80s
Plymth Mgr '90-92
Palace Asst Mgr '95

Portsmouth Asst. '99-00

Oxford Mgr '00-01
Stoke '04-05
Plymouth '05-06
Stoke '06-13
Asst Mgr/Coach/Scout
Palace '14-14
Technical coach

"DES"
(Mark O'Connor)

Rovers '84/5
B'Mouth '85-90 Player
Gills '90-93
B'Mouth '93-95
Gills '95-99 Coach
P'Mouth '00-05
Plymouth '05-06
Stoke '06-13
Bristol C '13-

"TONE"
(Tony Pulis)

Rovers '74-84 P'Mouth '80
B'Mouth '86-89 Stoke '02-05
Gills '89-90 Plymth '05-06
B'Mouth '90-94 Stoke '06-13
Gills '95-99 Palace '13-14
Bristol C. '99-00

"LINDS"
(Lindsay Parsons)

Rovers '64-77 (player)
Yth Coach 80s
Cheltenham '92-95
Gills '95-'99 Asst Mgr
Bristol C '99-80
P'Mouth 2000 Coach
Stoke Scout
Plymth '05-
Stoke '07-13

+ "Rudgey"
(John Rudge).

Rovers player '72-75
B'Mouth player '75-77
Stoke '99-13 Dir of Football.

+ "Badger"
(Gerry Francis)

Palace player '79-81
Rovers Manager '85-91
Stoke coach '08-12
Palace coach

"ADIE"
(Adrian Pennock)

B'Mouth '92-96
Gills '96-03 (Player)
Stoke '07-13 (Coach)
Forest Green '13-

+ "Reidy"
(Peter Reid)

Stoke Asst Mgr '09-10
Plymouth Mgr '10-11

+ "Gaz"
(Gary Megson).

Plymouth player '77-79
Stoke Manager '99
Stoke coach '07

what his "Director" role actually consisted of. In truth, Tony had a lot to thank Rudge for, particularly in his early days, although other gang members soon "overlapped" some of Rudgey's workload.

Others who also passed through the gang were Peter Reid and Gary Megson, but the main addition in 2008 was Gerry Francis, the former Bristol Rovers, Spurs and QPR manager.

Gerry had effectively been retired for several years when he got the call, and he needed a bit of persuasion: "I didn't really know Tony but he asked if I'd come in. I said I'd do it for one year - and ended up there for five years. I come in on a Tuesday and Thursday to work with Tony. When I first started there we were sat in portakabins, and some of them leaked. Then I go to all the games. I sit up top where you do get a better view much quicker - I ring down to the dugout what I see and then it is up to Tony. The most important thing is what is happening on the field. The priority has to be the first team, performances and results."

With his gang working hard behind the scenes, Tony was able to concentrate more on that priority, particularly that first team.

Bambi On Ice

Although Tony had started spending Coates' money the previous season, he had still balanced the books. His sale of the likes of Michael Duberry had raised nearly £1.5m, more than he spent on the likes of Fuller, Lawrence and Higginbotham. The same went for the 2007/08 season when he released his favourite Higginbotham for £2.5m (it was too good an offer) to Sunderland and his less-favourite Carl Hoefkens to WBA for £750,000. Cynical supporters reckoned this was typical Tony Pulis, throwing away the real talent, and thus any real chance of success.

But it allowed him to splash out on a goal-scoring defender, Leon Cort (a record £1.2m), a striker Richard Cresswell (c£300k) whom Tony played so deep and wide that he rarely seemed to make it to the opponents' penalty area, a sweeper-midfielder Glenn Whelan (£500k) who was soon called up by Ireland, and a giant forward called Jon Parkin (£225,000), better known as The Beast – what better name for a Pulis-striker.

One of his most shrewd signings, though, was a 19-year-old Manchester United reserve defender called Ryan Shawcross, but Ryan admitted later that he was actually heading elsewhere. "To be honest I was going to join another team on loan, but he [Tony] wouldn't let me out his sight till I signed, which pretty-much sums up Tony Pulis. He told me I'd be starting on the weekend, and so that was it for me. I got my first game and scored, and that was that. He's a great manager and he's done fantastic for me."

Tony concurred that he had to work hard to get Ryan on board: "He could've gone off to Norwich or Ipswich, who were above us in the standings at the time. But I managed to convince him that what we were doing here was the right thing for him and that we were going to be successful."

Tony receives warm welcome at Bristol City

Initially Tony took him on loan as if he needed convincing that this still-growing bean-pole had what it took to be a Pulis-defender. "He was like Bambi on ice," Tony later described him. But when he scored on his debut in a 1-0 win in the opening game of the 2007/08 season at Cardiff, Tony was convinced. He went on to score 6 more before New Year, by which time his partner in central defence, Leon Cort, was also putting them away just as fast (8 goals each for the season). In the January 2008 window, £1m secured Bambi's services from Alex Ferguson.

With a decent set of signings, and goals beginning to flow from all parts of the team – Fuller and Lawrence in particular – even cynical fans began to sit up and take notice. The last nail in the protest movement came in late-September 2007 with the visit of Holloway's Plymouth and their still-bitter supporters. Despite going 4 games without a win, Stoke went 1-0 up, but then 1-2 down to two ludicrous goals. It resulted in a chorus of "Pulis, Pulis, what's the score?" first from Plymouth supporters and then from a large number of Stoke fans. This time goals from Lawrence and Fuller won the game at 3-2. It allowed Tony the luxury to address the moaners with sarcasm after the match by supposedly apologising for only being 5th in the table with such a threadbare squad. He'd made his point.

Whether the doubters liked it or not, Stoke under Tony Pulis really looked like they really were going places...well, make the playoffs anyway this season. But then anything less would be seen as failure.

There was one aspect of Tony's team that was to define his style for the next few years. Rory Delap returned from injury, and despite being a solid and tireless midfielder, he revealed there was another string to his bow: a long-throw so fast and powerful that it could travel at a low horizontal trajectory like a cross or a corner, rather than looping high into the air like a lob.

Tony wasn't actually the first to pick up on it. Delap, who unsurprisingly had been a schoolboy javelin champion, started using his party-piece at his very first club. "At Carlisle I'd do it in the last 10 minutes or so if we weren't winning. It was the same at Southampton, but Derby used it to get in behind the defence rather than throw it into the box."

Tony lost for words after seeing Rory throwing

Of course, the long-throw wasn't everybody's cup of tea: "Sunderland didn't use it. It works sometimes. One hundred throws might create two goals – it's like corners and free-kicks."

But the difference at Stoke was that Tony Pulis put the throw at centre stage, turning it into an art form and Delap into a minor celebrity. "The thing that was different about Stoke was that it was such a tall team, which obviously helps with throw-ins. At over six foot I was one of Stoke's smallest players and we probably had seven or eight strong headers of the ball. It meant that from throw-ins we always had four or five effective attacking options in the box at the same time. Most teams have three or four at most."

To Tony it was another way of getting the ball into the box. If the team were struggling to get forward, particularly away from home, it was a way to take the heat off the defence, create chances up front, ...and generally terrify the opposition. As Tony astutely observed: "Even Portsmouth, who have a big side, every time Rory threw the ball in they were frightened to death. It's a great weapon for us and we'll continue to use it, irrespective of whether people like it or not."

Seven goals were attributed to Delap's throw for the 2007/08 season,

10% of Stoke's haul that season. Five of the goals were scored at home, where the increasingly noisy Stoke crowd turned each throw into a rousing event.

Soiling The Game

What soon became evident was that Stoke were more than a match for the top Championship sides. Only on his return to that intimidating

Ashton Gate ground, where he'd made his debut all those years ago, did Tony come a cropper, losing 0-1 to Bristol City. But slowly Stoke made progress from mid-table to play-off positions, although it was clear that many (particularly in the media) were not taking them seriously.

It all came to a head in the home game against top-of-the-table West

Tony still lost for words after seeing Rory throwing

Brom, 3 days before Xmas 2007. Stoke, now up to 4th spot, already had an astonishing record against Albion over the previous 20 years, but their manager Tony Mowbray insisted that his team were the more successful playing proper attractive football.

That day, Stoke annihilated The Baggies by 3-1 in one of their best performances for decades, with Fuller scoring a brilliant hat-trick, the first treble at The Brit for 7 years. It knocked West Brom off the top, and laid out Stoke's high ambitions for the future.

But it was not well-received. The media refused to accept that the darlings of the Championship had been beaten fairly and squarely by a better, more organised side. All Mowbray could say was "I saw what I saw...I saw my team playing some decent football." Others were not so nice, with The Birmingham Mail describing Stoke City as "big and as ugly as sin", claiming they could only praise Stoke through gritted teeth. They said they found it difficult to compliment a side relying on percentages as much as an accountant, and a side who were simply soiling the game! They even went as far as to suggest that Tony would be receiving a table football set for Christmas, with 9 players on the back pole defending and hoofing the ball forward. Charming.

Even the sympathetic Guardian reported that Stoke's misfortune was that "they continue to be damned with faint praise", noting that it was Albion's goal that was the "ugliest" of the afternoon, whereas Fuller's was as sweet as a nut.

But then Tony didn't care what they said, much to the delight of Stoke fans. "I honestly don't give a damn what people outside Stoke say about Stoke City. We all pull together, it's a great football club, great group of supporters. People outside may moan and groan, but who gives a damn!"

"We've matched West Brom with commitment, energy, good pace and power and a togetherness that has pushed this club forward." And it was working off the pitch as well, as Tony revealed about his hat-trick hero: "It's the first time in two spells I've been manager that the club has gone to a player who has got 18 months left and offered him a new contract."

Just over the next hill

With the strange sight of Mama Sidibe scoring, and the team coming back from 0-2 down to bottom club Scunthorpe to win 3-2 (Tony's half-time talk supposedly blistered the paint off the changing-room walls), Stoke went top of the table in February 2008. But then Tony won Manager Of The Month again, and as a result March (as March often is) was a disaster.

With one win in 8 games (a Sidibe scored 1-0 win at Norwich), Stoke clung on to a promotion place, despite even losing 1-2 at home to playoff hopefuls Crystal Palace. Thankfully most of the other promotion chasers didn't enjoy March much either.

The moment of truth was Stoke coming back from 0-1 down at struggling Coventry. After another rousing half-time team talk from Tony, a recalled Fuller scored from the spot, and super-sub Lawrence hit the winner before ripping off his shirt like a modern day Adonis. Stoke pushed Bristol City off the top-spot with 3 games left.

Appropriately, Bristol visited Stoke for the next game, but Sidibe saw them off with a sparkling first-half brace in front of the Sky cameras. The game finished 2-1, informing the TV world that the City most likely to go up was from Stoke not Bristol. And there was much gnashing of teeth!

With the much-maligned Cresswell scoring the winner (it was actually his 12th of the season) in the penultimate game at Colchester (1-0), it looked like promotion had been achieved after 90 minutes. West

Brom had used up their games-in-hand and were destined to be champions, but a late run by Hull City was the major threat, particularly when their late winner against Palace meant that Cresswell's goal wasn't going to be enough. Stoke needed another point in their final game to be sure of promotion. It set up a nail-biting home game against Leicester City who needed a win to avoid dropping to the third tier for the first time in their history.

The date of the last game was the 4th of May...or Star Wars Day as it's better known.

"May-The-Fourth Be With You!"

Tony Pulis had been promoted twice before, once as a player and once as a manager.

Tony's bus-top promotion celebration. He had now been promoted from all three lower divisions

As a player he was promoted with AFC Bournemouth. They gained promotion by winning at Fulham in their penultimate game on...May the 4th.

As a manager he was promoted with Gillingham, with the club celebrating promotion with a 1-0 win over Scarborough in their final game on...May the 4th.

Now on this May The 4th, Tony was playing against his old mate Ian Holloway, who somehow had got sucked into a relegation battle. Ian had left Plymouth and joined Leicester, and boy, did the Plymouth supporters hate him for that, barracking him far more than they ever did Tony.

And who should be Chairman of Leicester? Only Tony's old boss at Portsmouth, Milan Mandaric, whom Tony had sued to get his contracted money. Mandaric, who hadn't missed a Leicester game all season, decided he would sit this one out, citing pressing business in the USA and also "family commitments". "Certain matters could not wait any longer," he claimed.

The actual game itself ended 0-0 and certainly wasn't a classic; as

Hull lost at Ipswich, the result was irrelevant to Stoke anyway. But 25,000 Stoke fans invaded the pitch at the end, ecstatic that their club was back in the top-flight for the first time in 23 years. Stoke City under Tony Pulis were in the Premier League. Nobody could really believe it. As one fan put it: "It's soooo good to be a Stokie. Can't write anymore at the moment – too excited. Sooo happy!"

For Tony, though, it was the big time for him and Stoke. For Milan Mandaric, it was a just a bad time.

"It is a dreadful experience," Mandaric said. "Right now I am not a very happy man. It is not an easy moment. It is one I have never experienced before in any project, whether business or football. You don't have to be Einstein. If you look at the support I have given to my managers and my players, both financially and morally, and what do you get in response? You expect rewards and results. We didn't get it and you have to feel let down. We owe it to the supporters to turn this around and find some positives in this dreadful time." Sadly, he'd burnt his bridges and couldn't even turn to his old mate Tony for help.

Tony and Milan - what could possibly go wrong...?

Curiously, it was something Ian Holloway said about Leicester's performance that summed up Stoke's right to promotion. "If I had seen performances like that all season, we wouldn't have been where we are," he said. Clearly, Stoke were light years above this Championship standard. Tony had made them organized and disciplined (even Fuller to a certain extent!). It was no fluke, they deserved promotion.

"I've had promotions before as a manager and player," Tony admitted, "but in those days you'd get a gathering outside the town hall or whatever. But in Stoke all kinds of people were coming out of their front doors, standing on cars, waving from bridges...truly terrific!

"This team and this season will go down in history in these parts. The players have got to soak up times like this because they don't come round very often in your average career or lifetime."

Whether they had a hope in hell of staying up was another matter.

Chapter 6 – The Big Time (2008-2011)

Part 1 – "Doing-a-Derby"

Everyone was really delighted in 2008 to see Tony Pulis' Stoke City in the Premier League...well, if they were Stoke fans, they were. Everyone else was filled with the sort of horror that is usually saved for "slasher" movies and letters from the taxman.

The snobbery of the so-called elite of English football resulted in a huge backlash against Tony and his methods before a ball had even been kicked. In their eyes, the "New Wimbledon" had just arrived, and...Oh look, they've learnt a new trick: a long throw. How simply ghastly! They were going to be given short-shrift, that was for sure.

Unsurprisingly, Tony didn't care at all. In fact he revelled in it. As less and less was expected of him, this attitude actually worked in his favour as he eagerly mined the underdog seam. He even kept quiet about the fact that he'd spent part of the summer completing his UEFA Pro License.

So it was not surprising that although Stoke's first season in the Premier was remembered by fans (and media) for being exhilarating, emotional and most-of-all LOUD, ...it is almost forgotten that it was also alarmingly calamitous!

Show me the money

After the joyous scenes following promotion, reality soon kicked in at Stoke City in the summer of 2008. Derby County had just been relegated after one season in the top flight with a record low of only 11 points. The phrase "Doing-a-Derby" entered general use for clubs who just couldn't cope in the Premier. Many felt (and hoped) that this was the fate awaiting Tony Pulis.

One thing was for sure: Stoke were not staying up unless they seriously strengthened their painfully thin Championship squad. So, before you could say "Carl Dickinson", Tony had blown a staggering £22 million. In hindsight, most of it went straight down the drain. So much for the frugal years before promotion. But the idea was that Premier League rewards would soon recoup that...assuming they survived.

But the three jewels in Tony's crown were defender Danny Higginbotham (returning from Sunderland, £2.5m), iconic Abdoulaye Faye (rescued from relegated Newcastle for a snip, £2.2m), and heroic goalkeeper Thomas Sorensen (free, and a dam-site cheaper than the courted Scott Carson who bewilderingly at the last minute chose West Brom instead costing them a cool £4m).

But most attention fell on 28-year-old £5.5m Dave Kitson, a tall auburn striker from Reading. Much was expected of him, in particular a healthy trawl of goals. Of all his signings, this was the one Tony felt he would be judged on. "He's a proven goalscorer in the Premier League; they're very difficult to get those," claimed Tony, optimistically.

But with Kitson partnering Mama Sidibe up front in their opening Premier game at Bolton, Stoke were made to look like a Championship side still, going 3-0 down by half-time.

Ricardo Fuller came on to score Stoke's first Premier goal in the last minute, but the damage had been done. The odds on Stoke being relegated shortened dramatically overnight. They were being written off after only one game.

To add insult to injury, the betting firm Paddy Power pulled off a sneaky publicity stunt by paying out immediately to anyone who had already bet on Stoke to go down. In reality it was a cheap piece of advertising – it actually only cost them £30k AND it was a poke in the eye for Peter Coates' bet365 company.

However, this was right up Tony's street. "It was actually a real source of inspiration. It helped us immensely," he later revealed, and it galvanised the club and its fans as it prepared for its first home game, against a

Vincent Pericard preparing for that vital Hartlepool game

star-studded Aston Villa featuring Gareth Barry, Ashley Young, Gabriel Agbonlahor, Reo-Coker and Brad Friedel. Amidst carnival scenes at a heaving Britannia Stadium, Stoke pulled off an amazing 3-2 victory, with a spirited goal-of-the-season by Fuller followed by Sidibe's glance-header winner from a Rory Delap long-throw in the very last seconds. Tony's super-sub had done the trick: "Mama's a gem of a lad, and when you're bringing him on with 20 minutes to go he can be a handful, and he was." Tony's first Premier win was under his belt, and what a classic.

But however wonderful this game was – and it was – it was also clear that points were going to be very hard to come by. What followed were 4 defeats in the next 5 league games. Sandwiched in between these defeats was a stoic 0-0 draw at rampant Liverpool, which showed that on the day Stoke could hold their own against the top clubs.

Tony's plan was to take advantage of struggling clubs, such as the chaotic Spurs under Ramos, who were dismissed by 2-1, as was Gareth Bale after only 20 minutes. And of course they had the secret weapon in Rory Delap's long throw that had so much power it seemed to zing over horizontally like a rocket. For the second season in a row, it proved effective.

Although the long-throw could hardly have been called a secret, clubs such as Sunderland were fooled by it – Fuller heading home a Delap special late on for a 1-0 win. But the sight of Arsene Wenger's tiny-looking Arsenal side being so unprepared for the long-throw onslaught was bewildering, as his side were beaten by 2-1 (with both goals from long-throws). Even better, Robin Van Persie got so frustrated that he barged Sorensen and got red carded. Wenger's moaning about Stoke's rough tactics (despite the sending off of his own player) and long throws (maybe they should be banned??) began a long (albeit light-hearted) feud with Tony and Stoke fans.

Tony just laughed it off: "In life you do the best you can with what you've got. I've got no gripes with what people say. I get annoyed if other clubs criticise us as a club, but personally I try not to let it affect me. I can't affect what Wenger thinks so I don't worry about it. We all need to stop worrying about things we can't affect. We worry ourselves into our graves."

But it wasn't all plain-sailing. Manchester United were less forgiving, humiliating Stoke by 5-0 with goals from their star players Ronaldo, Carrick, Berbatov and Welbeck. It was a real wake-up call for Tony, and showed up the chasm between the top and bottom of the Premier. Stoke recovered to scrape a 1-0 win against West Brom – another late winner for Sidibe – but as the winter arrived things began to get desperate.

From mid-table safety, Stoke spiralled down into the relegation zone with an 11 game winless streak, whilst only managing a miserable 6 goals. They also began picking up unnecessary red cards. Fuller's at West Ham was a particular classic. His sending-off for slapping his own captain Andy Griffin after the Hammers equalised was particularly perturbing. With Stoke sharing bottom place with West Brom and Middlesbrough, it was clear that Tony had to pull something out of the hat. Better managers had lost their jobs at this stage of the game.

Gambling on Etherington

The turning point, or perhaps the wake-up point, was the FA Cup exit at Hartlepool. Tony proudly fielded most of his expensive signings from the previous August, some of whom had barely had a game all season. They included Andrew Davies (£2m from Southampton), Ibrahima Sonko (£2.25m from Reading), Tom Soares (£1.25m from Crystal Palace), Seyi Olofinjana (£3m from Wolves), Michael Tonge (£2m from Sheffield United) and the luckless Dave Kitson (£5.5m).

A merry Tony Pulis at the Hartlepool pre-match press conference.

With £16m worth of new signings on display (and, er, ex-Juventus player Vincent Pericard) Stoke lost pitifully by 2-0, revealing a real lack of quality in the Stoke squad. Worse, Kitson couldn't even score against a League One side; the striker that Tony had pinned his hopes on went on to finish the season goalless.

But with his back firmly against the wall, Tony pulled off a master stroke in the January window, picking up left-winger Matthew Etherington (£2m from West Ham) and striker James Beattie (£3.5m from Sheffield United). Both came with baggage, particularly Etherington's gambling problems in the tabloids. "I blew £1.5m on gambling and kept my shame a secret from family!" was a typical headline. Tony brushed off the knockers by claiming that when it came to recruiting players, Stoke had fewer options, being "more of a Battersea Dogs Home than a Crufts".

What sealed Stoke's fate was Tony finally recognising that his best combination at the back (and, by God, he'd tried them all and more) was the powerful partnership of Ryan Shawcross and Abdoulaye Faye. He cemented this by making the man-mountain Faye the new team captain. As The Oatcake put it "How on earth did we pick him up for just £2m?"

The crunch game came in January against Manchester City, the first time Beattie partnered Fuller, who was returning from suspension. With the Brit roar turned up to 11, and Stoke down to 10 – another red card, this time Delap for kicking the ball at Wright-Phillips – Stoke turned the corner with an inspired performance. The winning goal was appropriately an extraordinary Beattie header from an Etherington cross.

Stoke slowly carved out the results that would rescue them from the relegation zone. Two very late goals by Ryan Shawcross and Glenn Whelan earned them a point at a startled Villa Park, and home wins against Bolton (2-0) and Middlesbrough (1-0) were vital.

Abdoulaye, My Lord...Le coeur d'un lion

But on the 4th April, Stoke finally got what long-suffering travelling fans thought they'd never see – a Premier away win. Fuller and Beattie's goals were more than a match for who-else-but West Bromwich Albion. The Potters even miraculously managed a second away win, a storming 2-1 victory at Hull. But it was Stoke's performances at Fortress Britannia that most fans will remember, and the extraordinary bear-pit atmosphere that it created. Pronounced the loudest fans in the land (123 decibels, louder than a pneumatic drill), home supporters enjoyed 10 wins and only 4 defeats from 19 games, figures that had a lot to do with what Tony christened "Our 12th Man". Many clubs came a-cropper, and some even had the nerve to complain about it: "It just makes me laugh [when] teams come to the Britannia and our grass is half an inch longer. The pitch is within regulation but smaller and they moan if they lose. That pitch is the same size as Goodison Park!"

Stoke signed off with a 4-1 defeat at Arsenal in front of 60,000 supporters, but it didn't matter. They had finished in a healthy albeit highly unlikely 12th spot with 45 points. As Tony observed, 12 months previously Stoke had been playing in front of a full-house at Colchester, an attendance only a tenth that of The Emirates. "The success we've had in the past two years has been pretty amazing and it is most probably the best period this club has ever had. To get promoted and survive in the Premiership when everybody had already written us off are indeed remarkable achievements." As The Times newspaper eloquently put it: "People have had streets named after them for lesser achievements."

It had been a rollercoaster of a season, and the fans were eager to ride it again!

She Stood There Laughing

After all the abuse aimed at Tony's supposedly negative style, the football world became a tad (but only a tad) consolatory towards him. It was begrudgingly accepted that his Stoke side had stayed up against the odds.

One of his fiercest critics had been the acclaimed Stoke writer Stephen Foster, whose first Stoke book, the excellent "She Stood There Laughing", charted Tony's first season with Stoke. Stephen coined the phrase "Pulisball", and wrote of the long-suffering fans having to endure it. He had a point, but then the 2002/03 season had been a fight for survival. In his second book, "And She Laughed No More", he was more philosophical, as he ploughed through Stoke's first season in the Premier League. At first he was an even fiercer critic of Pulisball, before mellowing, accepting there might be more to Tony's tactics than met the eye.

The contrasts between Stoke and the likes of Arsenal was that Stoke's players really did look like men not boys, as Alec Stock had told Tony they should. Watching the big Stoke players (and not just Jon Parkin!) with an assertive do-or-die attitude playing against squirrel-like boys, diving about and crying to the ref, certainly made watching The Potters seem a very manly pastime. It wasn't exactly a testosterone-fuelled experience, but whenever Tony used the expression "It's a man's game" – and, yes, he did so on many occasions – Stoke fans knew what he meant.

For example, when asked about the extraordinary moment when Andy Wilkinson was sent flying by a Sunderland player, and yet just got up and shook the other guy's hand, Tony said: "Because of the way I've been brought up, people had said you dust yourself down and get on with the game. It's a man's game; it's not a girl's game. And that's always stuck with me. As a young kid when you got hurt, you got up and showed you weren't hurt, until you got to the dressing room, where you could cry your eyes out if you wanted, but you couldn't show it on the pitch! That's the way I am, and I've never changed. I'm pretty traditional in that respect."

This red-blooded experience probably had as much to do with the fact that attendances at The Britannia Stadium rarely dipped much below the 27,500 capacity in Tony's Premier seasons.

However, an unlikely source for faint praise was on BBC's Match Of The Day, where Tony and Stoke were written off on a weekly basis as being one-dimensional. Long time fans of the programme from the Stoke area, and even Tony himself ("I rush home to watch Match Of The Day;

Tony pleased to be talking to the BBC

I've watched Match Of The Day since I was knee-high to a grasshopper," he famously told Gary Lineker) felt Stoke weren't getting the credit they deserved.

That was until March 2009 when Alan Hansen bullishly responded to Lineker, who'd described Stoke as "plucky": "I am a fan. A massive fan. For honesty, for work-rate, for making the best of what you've got, and not crying when things are going badly for you. It's a ten! I mean, Pulis has done a fantastic job there to keep them going." [The "crying" reference was aimed at Manchester United, who'd had Paul Scholes and Wayne Rooney sent off that day.]

When Stoke came back from 0-2 down at Villa Park, Hansen went further: "What he [Pulis] did was he started with Plan A – had flaws in it, didn't quite work. Then for 9 minutes in the 2nd half he went to Plan B, and that didn't work. So he went to Plan C, and it worked, and I think that's brilliant management. You've got a plan, you recognise it's not working; you go and try something else. But it was a Stoke performance, it had...it was just grit and determination, and that's what Stoke's all about, and they will fight and fight for their lives, and they're good at it...That is absolutely magnificent. That is great management!"

Even Mark Lawrenson had to concede that Stoke might even stay up: "You read about fans booing their own players," he observed. "I tell you what, *Never At Stoke!*"

Made In Wales

After all the barracking and protests, Tony had won over the Stoke crowd. As long as he kept producing the goods, he was their man. The more the outside world criticised, the more loyal the supporters seemed to become.

The older and more sage-like fans compared him to another unsung Stoke manager, Alan Durban. He too had come from South Wales, only 30 miles from where Tony was born, in fact. In 1978 Durban had taken over a struggling 2nd tier Stoke, gave them a serious reality-check, and got them promoted to the top-flight. Not only that, but he turned them into an established top side, poised for a possible place in Europe. And his basic approach was using big strong players, a physical game with a little bit of flair on the side, played out in front of a bear-pit of resurgent Stoke fans.

Famously, Durban also liked socking it to the press. Criticised for the negative approach of

It was either this or the steelworks.
Tony at Newport County.
Courtesy of South Wales Argus

(shock horror) playing 5 in midfield at Highbury after 3 awful away defeats in a row, Durban hit back saying, "If you want entertainment, go and watch a bunch of clowns!" What Durban actually said was: "If you want entertainment, you could go out and get a bunch of clowns. If obtaining pleasure from matches is the only concern, then you could get rid of coaches and let the players go out and get on with it." As The Observer newspaper sneered: "Well, there you go – but obviously not to Stoke unless you're a masochist." Tony would have been proud of that one.

Coming from South Wales, both Alan Durban and Tony Pulis were tough as old nails. But after saying that, they had both taken route one out of South Wales, and had made footballing successes of themselves, although it had taken Tony till he was 50 to reach the top-flight (for

Durban it was 27 as a player and 37 as a manager).

Tony's start had been humble: "My dad worked in the steelworks. There was eight of us in a three-bed house. When I later got the chance to go and play football and get paid I realised how lucky I was. I would

The honourary doctor from Staffs Uni

wake up not believing it." Tony took every opportunity to play when he was a 'kiddie'. "We played a lot of football in the streets and up against wooden doors. You can't play in streets now; too many cars on the road!" He and his mates moved on to a piece of waste ground down by the docks beside the railway tracks. They were soon joined for a game by dockers and steelworkers. "They'd had a few pints, and still had their steel toecaps on. They didn't hold back because we were kids; in those circumstances, you learnt quickly."

However, although Welsh through-and-through, Tony's grandfather had originally come over from Malta, although Tony's connection with the Mediterranean was purely football-related. Until recently the only time he'd visited the island was in the Spring of 1975 when playing for Wales in UEFA's European Youth Cup against Malta. Wales won 4-0 at Cwmbran, and 1-0 at the Empire Stadium in Gzira. Amazingly more members of his family (his distant relatives still living in Malta) were watching him in Gzira than had been at the first game in Cwmbran. Tony's Wales side then beat Poland 3-0 and drew with Italy 0-0 in the finals in Switzerland, before being knocked out 0-4 by Hungary. Inevitably England went on to win the competition.

But even Tony admits that over the years he has changed...a bit: "I'm actually a lot softer now than when I first started in management. Society has changed. Football has changed. The world has changed. If you don't change with it you'll get left behind, so we all have to adapt. But you still have to be in charge of the group, and there are times when you have to show you are in charge of the group."

"The biggest thing about management is self-motivation. The biggest thing about being in the Premier League, if you're a club like Stoke, is recognising that you are going to lose games on a fairly regular basis. If you can't handle that you are going to go under. You have to be strong."

"I have my grumpy days. The players will tell you that. But you have to be positive because you have to lift them."

Part 2 - Pushing On

If ever there was a Stoke season for prima-donnas under Tony Pulis, then 2009/10 was it.

Stoke's second season would turn out to be Tony's best ever league-wise. But it is more famously remembered for a blazing dressing-room row between Tony and striker James Beattie after losing 0-2 at Arsenal in December 2009.

The row had little to do with the game, and more about the details of a Christmas party the Stoke players had organised in London that weekend. Tony wanted them back in training early after the poor result, but this would seriously cramp the style of the partygoers wanting to make a weekend of it. Surely this had already been agreed, or was it just assumed?

Beattie wouldn't let it lie, and when Tony came charging out of the shower, allegedly naked (well, he wasn't known to shower in his tracksuit and cap) the row was cranked up a notch. How much physical contact there was after that will have to wait for another book (or possibly a film). More importantly, details of the row were surreptitiously leaked by another player, and the media had a field-day. Despite being a hero the previous season, Beattie started only ONE league game after this fiasco, before moving to Rangers in the summer.

Another striker soon on his way was Dave Kitson. He FINALLY scored a goal for Stoke, a whole year after joining Stoke for £5m, in the 1-0 victory against Sunderland. The Brit went mad with mirth, and even Tony rather optimistically predicted 10-15 goals for him; he only managed 5, including one against Orient. As things turned sour, he was described in the press as "petulant", particularly after being sulkily substituted in the 7-0 defeat at Chelsea. He was subsequently part-exchanged along with Liam Lawrence for Marc Wilson, and headed for Portsmouth.

But of all the prima-donnas, the most entertaining was Tuncay Sanli. Tony caused quite a stir by signing the talented striking-midfielder from relegated Middlesbrough in August 2009 in a £10m deal that included German defender Robert Huth. The Sentinel's Martin Spinks immediately saw a problem: "Where on earth do you play Tuncay?" or in other words: "What on Earth is Tony Pulis going to do with a skilful player like him?" What indeed.

Tony did indeed struggle to find a position for both Tuncay and Huth. Initially, Huth replaced Andy Wilkinson at right back, as Abdoulaye Faye continued to partner Ryan Shawcross in defence. Tuncay had to be content with the odd substitute appearance, whilst Tony stuck with his tried-and-tested favourites. This was particularly evident when incredibly, during the mid-season, Mama Sidibe made 14 consecutive starts, whereas Tuncay only managed a total of 9 in the same period. Eventually, Tuncay's patience wore thin, and the press reported his "childish attitude" to being substituted, which drew boos from the crowd. Despite providing some exciting moments at Stoke – including coming on as a substitute and scoring a humdinger of a goal against Manchester United – he moved on to Wolfsburg the following season. This was poetic, or at least almost as poetic as The Guardian who compared his signing as being "in much the same way a socially aspirational 18th-century farmer might have imported at vast expense a clankingly useless Austrian harpsichord that nobody within 300 miles can play and which ends up being used to prop open the parlour door".

The Best That You Can Do

Now that the first season in the Premier was out of the way, Tony began to look for more challenges and records to break as Stoke settled into mid-table stability.

Of course there were plenty of exciting matches in 2009/10. But it was also the season that Stoke won FOUR times in London for the first time in their history! They won 1-0 at Upton Park, with a wonder-goal from super-sub Ricardo Fuller; 1-0 at Craven Cottage, with a late winner from player-of-the-year Matthew Etherington; 1-0 at Brisbane Road, with an extra-time cracker from goal-shy Dave Kitson; but best of all was the 1-0 win at White Hart Lane.

Stoke's October win at Spurs was only the club's second EVER win there - their only other was a 2-0 victory under Tony Waddington in 1975. It was one of Stoke's greatest games, and one of Tony Pulis' greatest football moments.

More importantly, it was his first ever win over his old boss Harry Redknapp!

After taming the likes of Crouch, Kranjcar, Lennon, Keane, Jenas and Pavlyuchenko, Stoke struck in the 84th minute. Fuller set off on a meandering amble down the right touchline. When he neared the corner flag he suddenly skipped inside through several startled defenders (including Wilson Palacios), slipped the ball in to Glenn Whelan who curled the ball into the far corner of the net. Even BBC's Alan Hansen described it as: "Sensational ... Absolutely magnificent ... One of the performances of the season."

Even Tony thought it was divine: "It was a great finish by Glenn, and then you're just hoping that one of their top players doesn't turn water into wine and score an equaliser. It was a massive 3 points for us."

After this remarkable result, it was felt that Stoke City under Tony Pulis had arrived for real, and was making inroads.

In a dress rehearsal for the following season's cup run, Stoke saved their best for the FA Cup, where they beat both Arsenal and Manchester City each by 3-1 in gripping games. They reached the sixth round for the first time in nearly 40 years, only to go out tamely to Chelsea.

Last home game of season 2009, ...with Mark O'Connor in tow

Other headlines included Stoke's 3-2 win against Fulham, when the rest of the country was closed due to snow and ice; Arsenal's Aaron Ramsey breaking his leg in a collision with Ryan Shawcross (although Arsenal fans seem convinced that it was attempted murder); and Salif Diao scoring a goal, his first in the Premier for nearly a decade! Tony Pulis admitted utter bewilderment of Diao's 91st minute winner in a 2-1 victory at Pompey: "I didn't know Salif had scored the goal until I got into the dressing room. I actually thought Mama Sidibe had scored it – that's how bad my eyes are. I still couldn't believe it when I was told. I don't think he's ever got past the halfway line before, never mind got into the opponent's box." A proud moment for a dedicated Pulis-player.

Stoke finished 11th with 47 points, their best finish in the Premier. In fact, their highest finish in 30 years. But no doubt the stat that impressed Tony the most was that Stoke had become only the 2nd club to better their first season in the Premier.

Defending is for life, not just for Xmas

It is generally believed that to be a Tony Pulis player you need to have been born with the defending gene that causes you to fall back when it's all-hands-to-the-pumps. In fact it is a skill that can be drilled into you.

Although the set up and tactics of Tony's sides give the clear indication that the aim of the game is simply to not concede, there is some science behind the theory. Most important to know is that 85% of all goals are scored from INSIDE the penalty area (give or take 1% or 2%). Logically, if you stop the ball being struck in your own penalty area, half the job of winning is done.

Of course this 85% is an average for a whole season for all clubs. (4762 goals out of 5626 total for Premier League, 4709 of 5590 in Serie A, etc). One of the only places that this 85% figure is lower (down to a measly 82%) is in Brazil where they score more long range shots.

Each club can massage these figures a little by simply defending differently, by training to block long-range shots or packing the penalty area. But achieving both requires skill, organisation and...'ard work. As a result Tony's disciplined sides are usually amongst the top-clubs for fewest goals-conceded.

At Stoke, Tony's strategy for the rare chance of a goal scored from OUTSIDE the area (as only 15% of goals are scored like this) was to simply get a 'stopper', such as Dean Whitehead (another Sunderland signing), to block them. However, most frustrated opponents were reluctant to shoot anyway as they usually couldn't actually see the goal, as there were 8-10 Stoke players in the penalty area in front of them, along with 3 or 4 of their own players hoping-against-hope to receive the ball.

The 8-10 Stoke players would be there because if 85% of goals are scored by opposing players shooting or heading from INSIDE the penalty area, then (Tony reasoned) the best strategy was to stop opposing players from receiving the ball INSIDE the penalty area. All passes were to be blocked, mainly by just having overwhelming numbers of defenders; and when crosses rained in, Pulis had his tall defenders (Shawcross, Huth, Faye, et al) to head clear.

Tony's training sessions would reflect this, with piggy-in-the-middle type challenges on special mini-pitches, where sets of players have to stop the ball getting through them.

This explains why in most games Stoke defended deep. This resulted in the opposing team having more of the ball – anything up to 70% in some games, but nonetheless games that Stoke often gained points in. This often manifested itself as 10 Stoke defenders under siege refusing to be drawn out, unless by a sloppy pass leading to a counter attack. Stoke fans could scream "out!" till they were blue in the face, desperate to draw the Stoke players out of the penalty area to push back the opposition; but the players had their orders, because Pulis had the stats. And on the whole it worked.

As for Stoke defenders stopping the opposition from heading the ball from a set piece (usually a corner), as the ball was about to be lofted into the penalty area, something akin to a playground scuffle would occur. Again it was meticulously practiced on the training ground, and was in many ways like watching a beautifully choreographed ballet...or a skilful American-Football 'play'...or, well, just a playground scuffle.

Signing on for Wembley...and The World!

Some people have retrospectively criticized Tony Pulis for his reckless spending in his latter days at Stoke. But apart from The Potters' first season in the Premier League, most of his signings could be seen as quite shrewd (but we'll come to Wilson Palicios in a moment!).

His taste for experienced players often received the same criticism that Tony Waddington had shouldered in the 1960s for signing 'old crocks'. And then there was his attempt to suck Sunderland dry of all its players – Delap, Lawrence, Higginbotham, Whitehead, defender Danny Collins, and to cap it all, striker Kenwyne Jones (again). Even Sorensen was ex-Sunderland. It would often attract chants of Mackem-rejects from North-Eastern fans.

Tony also had to find a gifted-yet-awkward player to replace Beattie, and this manifested itself as the extraordinary winger, Jermaine Pennant. Mark Wilson fulfilled the player-playing-out-of-his-normal-position role, arriving from Portsmouth in a very generous swap for Lawrence AND Kitson AND some cash. Finally, Tony had to put in a copper-bottomed Pulis-player, someone playing the Sidibe-rôle, willing to work his socks off for the cause, yet be in the front-line for the flak; this resulted in £2.75m for Jonathan Walters from Ipswich.

Of course, it didn't stop fans pulling his leg, as the following transfer-window tweet showed: "Keiron Dyer - Injury-prone, ex-England international who never plays - released and looking for a new club.

Quick, somebody nick TP's phone!"

Certainly, a record Stoke fee of £8 million (albeit spread over 4 years) for 25-year-old Kenwyne Jones sounded a lot, but with most of his strikers aging or disappearing (eg. Tuncay, Beattie, Kitson), Tony needed to make a statement of intent. That statement read: "Kenwyne is unplayable on his day which is why this is a fantastic signing for this club." People sort of knew what he meant, but just to be sure he went on: "We need goals and we need strong competition among our strikers if we are to continue improving at this level. Kenwyne will give us that. It's no secret that I am one of his biggest admirers."

Kenwyne even took a "significant" pay cut in order to fit in with Stoke's wage structure, although it was admitted that Sunderland assisted with this just to ease him off their wage bill. "We work very hard on the structure at this club, especially wages," Tony explained, "and there was no way we could do the deal unless it conformed with those."

Even £2.75m for Walters seemed considerable, particularly for someone who had only ever made 4 Premier appearances, and that had been several years before, followed by a stretch in lower-league football.

But with the huge and increasing income from the Premier League pouring into a club with significantly fewer financial overheads than most – certainly compared to other Premier sides – it was natural for Tony to be spending this sort of money. Furthermore, his four main signings for the 2010/11 season – Kenwyne, Pennant, Walters and Wilson – all played a major role a few months later in a classic gig at Wembley.

Welcoming these new top players in 2010 was not a few leaky portakabins and some old dog-messed parkland, but a smart new state-of-the-art training ground with parking bays for all the Ferraris and Porsches. Costing a modest £5m and sporting a striking stainless-steel frontage, it soon became Tony's pride and joy, and even won an architectural award. It was perfect for attracting the best players. He would even have something nice to say about its treatment room: "That's where the players go for their cuddles."

Meanwhile, 30 miles up the M6 motorway, Manchester City were also signing a number of players for the 2010/11 season, including the likes of Yaya Toure (£24m), Aleksander Kolarov (£19m), James Milner (£26m), David Silva (£25m), and Mario Balotelli (£24m). They would all play a major part in a Wembley gig with Tony's new signings later that season.

When Tony was later asked after a Man City defeat what the difference between the two teams was, his glib reply was: "About £220 million." Not so much a gap, more a chasm.

Family guy

Not a week would go by at Stoke City press conferences when Tony didn't use the word "family".

Mainly he would use the word in reference to the club's owners. No more did he just name-check his friend and chairman Peter Coates; now he would refer to the board as "The Coates Family", in a way that almost sounded like he'd been prompted to do so. His relationship with other members of the family, such as Coates' children Denise and John who by now ran much of the family business, was always thought to be cooler than his close bond with their father, and this was only natural. Further, there were always rumours that Peter Coates was going to step down due to his age, with either the children taking over or selling up.

Tony even ran extensive checks on his beloved Mama

But Tony always spoke affectionately and respectably about the Coates family, emphasising the importance of the close bonds of "family". If they had disagreements, they were kept firmly behind closed doors.

Occasionally he would talk about his players' families, and even their "kiddies", as he would refer to them. It was clear that he preferred and respected players who were settled down and planning families, rather than those who drove round nightclubs drunk and disqualified. Tony was even known to "interview" the WAGs. Bineta Sidibe remembers being checked to see how settled Mama's family life was and whether she was a good influence! [If Tony had read about the hijinks in Mama's recent book 'The Luckiest Man In Football!', one wonders if he would ever have signed him!]

But Tony's own family was the most precious, with his parents in Wales and his wife and children in Dorset. "My wife has never wanted to move. I have a place up here [near Crewe] and I go back [to Poole] when I can but she's right: football can be a precarious business and it was better to bring up the kids in one place." In fact his wife, Debbie, had moved. It was widely reported that they'd bought a house for £4.2m in ultra-exclusive Sandbanks to live next to his friend Harry Redknapp, and there was much furore about his earnings and wealth as a result. In reality they had actually just moved house from Bournemouth to an area of Poole called Lilliput, around the harbour from Sandbanks. As Debbie observed, his home is a haven away from the limelight: "He doesn't bring any football problems home at all. As soon as he's in through the door, he switches off straightaway. He's a warm family man...he's not changed at all."

But fans usually don't consider that football managers have families, and the worries and concerns that go with them. One of the few exceptions in Tony's career was at the very start of the 2010/11 season, the worst start that any of Tony's club sides had ever made.

After 3 straight defeats – at Wolves 1-2, where new signing Kenwyne was carried off after only 12 minutes; against Spurs 1-2, where Sidibe was carried off after being on for only FOUR minutes; and at Chelsea 0-2, where local-hero Andy Wilkinson lasted a respectable 51 minutes before hobbling off – Stoke faced managerless Aston Villa at The Brit in a Monday evening televised game. A 4th defeat would make it Stoke's worst start to a season for over 100 years.

But Tony wasn't there for the build-up to the game. His 74 year old mother passed away earlier in the day in South Wales with Tony present with his family. "It was a massive strain for me because you want to keep it private. I spoke to my staff before the game, then mum passed away and so I decided to come back. Stoke City is my passion and my love, and so I'm sure my mum would have wanted me to be at the game."

He watched the first half in John Coates' executive box, missing only the first 5 minutes. Watching the game from a box certainly wasn't his style – he even admitted to calling Coates first to check it was alright to do so!

With Stoke losing 0-1 at half-time, and looking leaderless, Tony came down and gave them a teamtalk to remember. "I had no intention of going down at half-time, but I just couldn't help myself. I think it was important the players knew how committed I was."

As he ran along to the dugout at the start of the second-half, he received a huge ovation from the Stoke crowd, and in an emotionally-charged atmosphere, Stoke came back to win 2-1, with a late equalizer from a Kenwyne header and even later winner from Huth, stabbing home in the 93rd minute. It was a very moving day for everyone.

Heading for the top

By the time of his third season in the Premier League, the football world had mellowed slightly towards Tony Pulis. But referees still seemed to see the worst in his players, with games beginning to see a number of inconsistent decisions.

Most glaring was Gary Neville in the 1-2 defeat at The Brit. On a yellow card for a first half scything of Etherington, he did it AGAIN just minutes later. Even Neville realised he'd cocked-up big-style, and he'd got to go. But the ref didn't even bring him over for a stern word, and the watching millions around the world were stunned. The Stoke fans were understandably dismayed, chanting: "If he played for Stoke, you'd send him off!" and they were not wrong. Two years previously Andy Wilkinson was sent off for a 2nd yellow in a close game where the ref failed to see Rooney elbowing Faye in the face and Ronaldo kicking out at 'Wilko'. As a result, a fortunate United won 1-0 with a late winner against 10-man Stoke.

Tony was in his element playing the underdog, and took every opportunity to remind the media that it was one rule for one and another rule for everyone else. "I find the whole situation disappointing week after week. Look at the incidents where our players are being booked or sent off, then compare them with similar incidents involving others that are going unpunished."

It also focused attention on the referees officiating over Stoke games. Rumours even went around that refs were training up by watching videos of spurious Stoke manoeuvres. Tony was incensed: "All we have ever asked is to be treated the same as everyone else but there are preconceptions about us that are unfair". Sure enough there were several more dodgy decisions, until it was felt (by the media, at least) that overall these things even themselves out, particularly after 2 awarded penalties in the 3-0 annual demolition at West Brom.

For the 2010/11 season, Stoke's home form was back at its best with 10 wins from 19 - only two other teams won more at home outside the top three, a fact that Tony was particularly proud of, describing it as "absolutely magnificent". This form included destroying the Merseyside clubs. First Roy Hodgson's star-studded Liverpool were beaten 2-0 with goals by Fuller and Kenwyne, Stoke's first win against The Reds for 26 years. Then Everton went down 2-0, Stoke's first win against The Toffees for 28 years. Tony was a hard act to knock, and he now had two more notches on his bed-post.

The atmosphere at The Britannia Stadium was still, as Tony described it, "rocking!" Better still were the 4-0 destruction of Newcastle (where the supporters loudly suggested that Joey Barton "kicked like a girl"), and another brilliant 3-1 tonking of Arsenal (where the fans responded to Arsene Wenger's suggestion that Stoke employed rugby tactics by chanting "2-0 to the rugby team" and "Swing Low Sweet Chariot").

One low point at home was defeat by Fulham by 0-2, which continued a spat between Tony and Mark Hughes. Hughes hadn't shaken hands with his opposite number after Stoke's 2-0 Carling Cup win, an act close to barbarism in Tony's eyes. So after this game, Tony slapped Hughes hand rather than shaking it properly.

Tony hypnotises an interviewer

Hughes just stood there looking insulted, a look he had perfected over the years when pretending not to understand something. Tony dismissed the whole thing: "It's two Welshmen with a bit of competition. I certainly won't lose any sleep over it and I'm sure he won't."

But away from home it was a different matter. Boxing Day 2010 saw Stoke achieve an impressive 3rd away success of the season, a 2-0 win at struggling Blackburn. Then the well ran dry. The Potters would not win away again in the league for 8 months. Away supporters began to feel that they were being short-changed by the way that Tony set out his teams away from home. It was seen as negative, and as defeat after defeat stacked up on the road, many of which were often dismal unadventurous affairs, fans made it clear that Tony needed to address this if only for the loyal fans who travelled so far. Their grumbles were masked by a remarkable Cup run, but that didn't mean the problem would go away.

Back to Wembley

Stoke City and the FA Cup had never gone well together. In fact, a 2009 study placed Stoke in lowly 90th position in their All-time-FA-Cup-Record, having won only a third of their 300-odd FA Cup ties. Above them were the likes of Crewe (83rd) and even Port Vale (38th)!

Aside from the FA Cup semi-finals of 1899, 1971 and 1972 – in all three ties City had taken the lead before going on to lose – Stoke were pretty awful in the FA Cup. Typical horrendous upsets included Rhyl (1-2, 1926), Walsall (0-2, 1966), Telford (1-2, 1992), Nuneaton Borough (0-1, 2000), and worst of all Blyth Spartans at The Victoria Ground (2-3, 1978).

Under Tony Pulis, there were few signs that The Potters were planning a dramatic cup run. The Hartlepool defeat in 2009 was not a total surprise. When Stoke were in the lower leagues, cup games were a chance to play and beat top-flight opposition. But with Stoke meeting and beating many of the top clubs in the Premier League, the FA Cup now seemed like an unwelcome distraction.

Tony always talked up the competition for historical and traditional reasons, but whereas in his playing days when cup games used to pack the grounds, now it seemed to empty them. But it did give him a useful opportunity to give fringe players the opportunity to get some games under their belt, and stop them knocking on his door. Ironically this now meant players such as goalkeeper Thomas Sorensen, who'd been usurped in October 2010 by rookie Asmir Begovic (signed by Tony on a scouting mission to Portsmouth supposedly to recruit veteran David James).

With a sparkling attacking squad – Etherington and Pennant on the wings, and Kenwyne and Walters in the centre – Stoke saw off Cardiff City (1-1, 2-0), Wolves (1-0) and Brighton (3-0), before being faced in the 6th Round by a West Ham side who had squashed them 0-3 the week before. In front of a near full-house, unusual for the FA Cup, Danny Higginbotham thumped a glorious free-kick through The Hammers' wall to clinch the winner in a 2-1 victory and send Stoke to Wembley.

Suddenly everyone at Stoke, including Tony Pulis, had to take the FA Cup seriously again. He was forced for once to put aside the fact that the club were only 4 points away from a relegation spot (they were 12th at the time) and 6 points short of the magic 40 points that he repeatedly claimed would keep them up for another season. What clinched it was his players rising to the occasion, delivering the dazzling 4-0 win against Newcastle the following week, closely followed by his first ever managerial point against Chelsea a few days later (1-1) with Walters racing the length of the pitch to score a wonder-goal. He could hardly complain.

The cup draw was kind, with the two mega-bucks Manchester clubs, City and United, paired in the first semi-final on the Saturday. Stoke would meet Bolton Wanderers on the Sunday.

This was only Stoke's 4th ever FA Cup semi-final. For Bolton it was their 14th! Also, Bolton, under media-darling manager Owen Coyle, were 6th in the Premier, playing attractive football, and going for a place in Europe. In comparison, Stoke were depicted as wearing hobnailed boots, kicking the ball long and wallowing just above relegation. If there was an underdog heaven, then Tony had gone there.

Tony celebrating loudly at Wembley

On the morning of April 17th 2011, just as in Tony's childhood footballing dreams, the motorways down to London were flooded with his club's colours. Inside the enormous new Wembley stadium, the sight and sound of the Stoke hoards with their sea of red and white flags and their Britannia roar were enough to exorcise Tony's demons from when he had last led a team out there, in the days Wembley had twin-towers.

But he had little to worry about. As opposed to Coyle, he'd stoked up his team up with fire and brimstone. It thus took only 11 minutes for Etherington to latch on to a loose ball and put Stoke 1-0 up. Then on 17 minutes, one of Tony's big defenders, Robert Huth, half-volleyed in the second. On the half-hour, Pennant put the sweetest pass through to Kenwyne to make it 3-0. As the fans danced and sang, Tony strutted along the touchline glowing with pride.

In the second half, when everyone was expecting a Bolton fight-back, Jon Walters ran through to hit a cracking 25-yarder for 4-0, before knocking in another for 5-0 a few minutes later.

Despite being almost hoarse after the game, Tony had just the right words for the occasion: "I'm delighted, I'm absolutely chuffed to bits."

The football world was dumbfounded. Now they couldn't ignore Tony Pulis. His side's victory was the largest for a senior team at the new Wembley stadium since re-opening, and the largest victory in any FA Cup semi-final since the War. They'd done it playing attacking passing football, with none of the goals scored from set-pieces or long-throws. And Stoke were going to the FA Cup final for the first time in their long history. Stoke fans shared Tony's ambition, which was: "I'll make sure I bloody enjoy it!"

What further barriers and records could this man break for The Potters? Well, two things came to mind. The first was winning the FA Cup final a month later, and the second was going into Europe, as the winner was entered into the Europa League.

Their Cup Final opposition would be the league's big-spenders, and Tony's Wembley-nemesis, Manchester City (who'd beaten United 1-0 in the other semi), then 4th place in the Premier. Tony had sworn never to return to Wembley after his bitter defeat at the hands of Man City, unless it was to lead out his team. Now he was up against them...again! Fate was playing cruel tricks.

A mural in Longton depicts the two Tonys on a par with one another

But intriguingly, even if the Sky Blues won the final, it would be Stoke City that would enter the Europa League in their place, as Man City would be entering the Champions League (assuming they finished in the top 4 of the Premier). It would cushion what many feared might be a heavy defeat to the rampant Mancini side.

What followed was another big day out at Wembley in May 2011, which did end in ultimate disappointment, although the millionaires Manchester City only just pinched it thanks to Yaya Toure's crashing strike from 15 yards late in the game. [Purists claimed that Carlos Tevez was offside, assuming he was interfering with play by obscuring Thomas Sorensen's view.]

The game was hardly a classic; to a neutral it was dire, with both sides' performances well below par in front of a 88,643 crowd. Stoke's only real chance was Kenwyne's 1-on-1 with Joe Hart which bounced off Hart's legs instead of through them. In truth Stoke were under siege for much of the time, and Manchester City missed some great chances, while Sorensen made some flying saves, including a fingertip effort to keep out a Mario Balotelli shot, which many observers rated as one of the finest seen at Wembley.

Losing 0-1 was still losing, and Tony was naturally disappointed. But he still spoke proudly of his players who had stood up against some of the greatest (or, as he put it, the most expensive) players in the world. The irony that he'd lost narrowly to Manchester City at Wembley again was not lost on him.

One excuse he might have milked more was the injuries to his squad. Whereas Stoke's physios had worked wonders over the years keeping his players on the pitch, his team was severely weakened on the run up to the Wembley games. First went hero Higginbotham, crocked against Chelsea; then Fuller's Achilles tendon went at Villa; Etherington dramatically tore a hamstring against Wolves; and Huth had an Arsenal player rather unnecessarily drop on his knee.

Tony surprisingly chose to play bandaged Huth and Etherington in the final, despite them clearly not being 100% fit, and Stoke supporters, who were also desperate for the duo to play, forgave him. They were team-players, he reasoned, but it didn't really do the team many favours, as the team were thus on the back-foot from the start.

What defender Abdoulaye Faye, overlooked after his stirring performance standing in for Huth the previous week in the 3-1 win against the mighty Arsenal, thought about this decision is anyone's guess.

This is the End, My only Friend

Memories can play tricks on people. When Stoke played in the FA Cup Final, a week before the last Premier League weekend, they were in 8th place with 2 games left. The first of those two matches was an embarrassing trip to Manchester City's Etihad Stadium just 3 days after their cup final defeat, losing again (0-3).

But the final game was at home to Wigan, who were desperate for points to avoid relegation. Despite every effort, and a disallowed Walters goal, Wigan mugged Stoke with a late winner, and celebrated survival into the night. Stoke thus finished 13th, 2 places lower than the previous year despite what was generally thought of as a decent season.

If the game had ended in a draw, then not only would Wigan have STILL been safe from relegation, but Stoke would have finished in the top half of the league for the first time in 36 years. It would also have given Tony Pulis that top-half finish that would prove so elusive and costly.

Chapter 7 – The Long Goodbye (2011-2013)

Part 1 – Hi Europe, meet Rory Delap!

Stoke's Europa League campaign of 2011/12 could arguably have been the catalyst for the decline of Tony Pulis at Stoke. It should have been the springboard for further success, but the side-effects of the Euro adventure were far reaching.

The first side-effect was the rapid enlargement of the Stoke squad. If the club were serious about making a dent in the Europa competition, they'd have to swell the ranks with quality players. The second was what effect it would have on Stoke's Premier status, seen (not just by Tony) as vital to the future of the club. The third was the hangover of its aftermath; would fans, board and media be able to live with the comedown after the excitement of a cup final and a European run?

ESPN give their take on Stoke's winning formula

Initially, all Tony had to worry about was getting his players back early for their Europa qualifying game against Hajduk Split in July 2011. Tony's tactics worked well, with a full-strength side gouging out two solid 1-0 wins against a staunch Split side in the face of some of the rowdiest fans in the world. If ever there was a case for Tony's discipline and preparation, this was it. But not everyone liked it. "I don't think it's right football," said the Split manager after watching Rory Delap. Tony response when he heard this was simply poetic: "I don't give a hoot, like I don't with anyone else!"

Stoke then saw off the rather more sedate Thun of Switzerland by 1-0 (a) and 4-1 (h), with the away leg being particularly remembered for Stoke fans conga-ing to "Doe, a deer, a female deer...". They were living the European dream, however surreal their interpretation of it was.

This meant that Stoke were through to the group stage, guaranteeing them 6 further games against even tougher opposition. Qualification meant that Tony had licence to expand the squad, but it left only 5 nerve-wracking days before the end of the transfer window.

However, the draw on the following day (26th August) revealed another challenge: to play in Kiev, Tel Aviv and Besiktas (none of which were traditionally thought of as, well, being in Europe). Stoke would have to travel nearly 6000 miles – thousands of miles further than other Europa clubs (although they were on a par with another club, FC Rubin, based 500 miles east of Moscow who were expected to fly in to play Spurs at a moment's notice) – for a selection of intriguing Thursday night games, squeezed in amongst all the other fixtures.

Crouchy and The Magician

Tony wanted a number of players fresh at home to cover for tired returning Europa players. He had brought in veteran defenders Jonathan

Potters pay £10m for Peter Crouch

...and he's worth every penny!

Fans were particularly pleased by the signing of Peter Crouch

Woodgate and Matthew Upson on short-term contracts, but then splashed out on exciting striker Cameron Jerome for £4m. This seemed a reasonable haul, but then, in cavalier style, he pushed the boat out and at the last minute spent £10m on legendary England striker Peter Crouch (his tallest signing to date) and £6m-£8m on midfielder Wilson Palacios, both from Harry Redknapp's Spurs and both on long 4 year contracts. The question was, had he over-reached himself?

Supporters were jubilant and the media got very excited, mainly about the late-night signing of 30-year-old Peter Crouch, who brought with him some badly needed European experience. Later, fans would point at his age and his 'sell-on' value as if they'd all suddenly become accountants; but for the time being they were impressed that Tony and the board were showing ambition, spending like other top Premier sides. It wasn't like the club couldn't afford it, they felt, with rich albeit prudent owners and an enormous Premier League income. Fans demanded stars and entertainment, and they got it, with Crouchy's goals beginning to flow. Tony would later say of him: "Signing Crouchy was a real statement of intent, and he's not let us down."

Tony now had 4 expensive strikers vying for 2 first team places, with 2 others (Fuller and Sidibe) in the wings. By Christmas, with the help of squad rotation, the plan seemed to be working, with Walters, Crouch and Kenwyne each with six goals. But Kenwyne's were mainly cup goals, and he and Jerome soon found themselves squeezed out, as Crouch eased into his permanent role up front, supported by ever-present Walters, who seemed to get the nod whoever was playing.

What was seriously unimpressive was Wilson Palacios. He looked unfit, he hardly played, and at times he didn't even look like a proper footballer. An extremely rare killer-through-ball would be followed by seemingly long spells of inertia. In Honduras he was known as The Magician, but Stoke saw no wizardry. A knee injury and tonsillitis were cited, but when Tony didn't play him one day because it was "too windy", questions started being raised. Whilst other clubs had resolutely refused offers from Tony for their players, a more willing Redknapp had at least agreed a deal with his old friend Tone. But were Crouch and Palacios bought separately, or was it a case of buy-both-or-none? Either way, Harry appeared relieved to have one or both of them off his hands.

Even Kempy couldn't explain the signing of Wilson Palacios

The reason so many questions were asked was because Tony prided himself on his signings and the research behind them. As the players were the products, or so he said, they had to pass the Pulis litmus test, and he took the vetting process very seriously. As he had stated years before about the thoroughness of his scouting research: "If I'm travelling, it's an ideal opportunity for me to see players away from home. I like watching players away from home as well as at home. I think there's a different atmosphere, and you see different characteristics away from home as well as some at home." (That certainly could be said for Tony's Stoke players.)

Most top clubs sign the odd player that doesn't gel. Even Tony'd had mixed success with signed players, particularly the group he'd signed on getting promotion in 2008. But at least there was every indication that Pulis-signed players had the determination to succeed, Dave Kitson being a good example. Wilson Palacios for a massive £8m didn't appear to fit this pattern at all, and soon set alarm bells ringing. Not many of those who watched him at Stoke would have argued when even The Sentinel summed up his time at Stoke as "miserable", with them going as far as to say that at times he was "nothing short of embarrassing" and (for £8m) "arguably the worst signing in the club's history".

Sunderland in disguise

With all the excitement of the new campaign, questions about these

Tony & George Andrews share a moment

signings would have to wait. Firstly, Tony had to mastermind the 2011/12 Premier League campaign. His rhetoric about dealing with a bad run of away performances was modified. Although it was clear that he wanted to address the issue, and maybe the larger squad might help here, he now implied that this would have to go on the back-burner whilst the club dealt with this season's new European challenges.

Subsequently, there were some pretty torrid experiences for travelling fans: 0-4 at Sunderland (3 days after gaining a 1-1 draw in Kiev), 0-5 at Bolton (3 days after a 2-1 win in Tel Aviv), 0-3 at Newcastle (Stoke's 52nd game of the season and running on empty. "Are you Sunderland in disguise?" the Toon fans helpfully enquired), 0-2 at Swansea (a particularly grim display, 3 days after beating Besiktas 2-1 at The Brit), and 0-2 at Wigan (described by The Oatcake magazine as "The Worst Performance Since Promotion...it really was that bad." So bad, they added harshly, that even Palacios coming on actually resulted in a minor improvement!).

Although some of the blame fell on the excess travelling some of the players had to undertake, arriving home at 5 or 6 in the morning, it was noted that many of the players who were left behind in Stoke underperformed all the more in the following games, either from being left behind or from lack of Pulis-time on the training ground.

Tony bought himself some breathing space as his team supplied some notable splashes of colour on the road: West Brom were mugged in the last minute with a comic goal where Ryan Shotton nipped in between dithering keeper and defender (making the record of only one defeat in 28 games in 23 years against the Baggies); Everton were beaten 1-0 at Goodison for the first time since 1981 ("What wins games is goals," explained David Moyes, patiently, "and they got the goal and we didn't."); Wolves were beaten at Molineux in the top flight for the first time since 1977 (a 2-1 win engineered by Tony subbing a calamitous Woodgate for an on-his-last-warning Pennant); and a feeble Blackburn side were suitably dismissed 3-1 (with Crouch curiously indicating his 100th league goal with his fingers). 4 away league wins plus a few credible draws (including 0-0 at Anfield) seemed a reasonable tally for such a tricky season. But for away fans the glass was still only half-empty.

Back at the Fortress

In the autumn of 2011, home fans got to see the threat of decent Europa sides seen off in an exciting sequence of games. Despite leading 0-1 in front of their noisy travelling fans, Besiktas went down 2-1 (Crouch and a Walters penalty). Maccabi Tel Aviv were beaten 3-0, which included Jerome getting sent off and then his nemesis Ziv getting red carded for a bizarre kicking-his-boot-at-the-linesman incident. Stoke then qualified for the knock-out stage by coming back late to draw 1-1 with Kiev, a classic Pennant cross for Kenwyne to head home. Thus Stoke became the only British club in 2011/12 to progress from the group stages to the last 32 of the Europa League. The likes of Spurs, Fulham, Celtic and Rangers didn't make it through, and although both Manchester clubs dropped down from the Champions League to the Europa League, they were soon knocked out too.

Other home glories included beating Liverpool 1-0 and drawing 0-0 with an AVB managed Chelsea. Best of all was defeating Harry Redknapp's high-flying Spurs TWICE at The Brit. Firstly they knocked them out of the Coca-Cola Cup with a 7-6 penalty shoot-out. Then Tony played all his ex-Harry/Spurs players to beat them 2-1, even bringing on Palacios in the last minute to rub salt in the wound. Spurs had just won

10 out of 11 games. It might have been this game when Harry decided to call Tony "a monster" in his subsequent autobiography. He may not have been such a monster, but he was certainly the master and no longer the pupil.

BBC's Juliette Ferrington presents Tony with a cake on his 10th anniversary

The crowning glory of the 2011/12 season was a single moment that justified the signing of Peter Crouch alone, a moment worth £10m of anybody's money.

It was in a March home game against league-leaders and multi-millionaires Manchester City. Just before the hour-mark and with the game still goalless, Begovic aimed a long clearance at Crouch, who duly headed it on to Pennant. Jermaine "with possibly his first header as a Stoke player" (so claimed The Sentinel's Martin Spinks) nodded it back for Crouch to tee it up. Crouchy then unleashed the mother of all volleys, manoeuvring the ball home from seemingly miles away & an impossible angle.

The Britannia Stadium erupted. In all their years nobody had seen anything like it (although some vaguely remembered a Jimmy Greenhoff goal 40 years earlier at The Vic). England's No.1 goalie Joe Hart was left fuming whilst the Stoke fans broke into a hilarious Poznan celebration at the stunned Man City fans. It almost didn't seem to matter to them that 20 minutes later Yaya Toure shot from what seemed like the next county, and the slightest deflection off Shawcross put it just beyond Begovic for 1-1.

Mancini's expensive bunch would go on to win the title on the last day in dramatic style, but they never scored a goal anywhere near as good. Tony could dine out on that goal for life, if he so wished. If Crouch's sell-on value was only going to be 57p and a bag of crisps, it wouldn't matter. That goal for Stoke City was priceless, and, as a result, the goal and the club went global.

Three wheels on my wagon

One thing that goal did do was to stop the media talking about Tony avoiding a driving ban two days earlier. Tony (and his BMW) had been caught doing 96 in a 60mph section of the M42 (Birmingham) on his way back from the 0-5 battering at Bolton. The fine was £2500 but it also meant 6 further points to his licence taking him to 15, past the driving-ban threshold of 12.

Amazingly, Tony was spared a ban as his defence lawyers had argued that if he had to employ a chauffeur instead that it would jeopardise his job and his club and many Stoke-on-Trent businesses and charities due to confidentiality reasons, as he drove and talked for 64,000 miles a year. "We signed Peter Crouch in the summer without anyone knowing," Tony told the magistrates. "That took almost four days of non-stop conversations between us and Tottenham and Peter and the like. If other clubs had found out, they would have been attracted and might have signed him before us. I have my staff whom I trust implicitly, but there are things I wouldn't even discuss with them."

The magistrates concurred, although they warned him he couldn't use that excuse again. It also didn't stop a certain reporter asking Tony the following day. "So, Tony, you've got 15 points on the road. Do you think you'll be adding to that this season?" At the time Stoke had won 4 and drawn 3 away from home. Tony barely batted an eyelid, and fluidly answered that with the evidence of recent away performances at Spurs (1-1) and Chelsea (0-1) he reckoned they would certainly be adding a number of points.

In fact the last four away games were pretty torrid, with only one point added to the tally. They included the aforementioned debacles at Wigan (0-2) and Newcastle (0-3), plus also Aston Villa (1-1, "Certainly no thriller at the Villa" observed The Oatcake), and finally QPR (0-1).

Tony seemed particularly dejected at losing the QPR game with the chance of sending them down. From his rhetoric it appeared to have something to do with QPR's manager Mark Hughes, who'd taken over from Neil Warnock. When asked before the game about his "fellow-Welshman" Hughes, you could almost hear Tony's teeth grinding. And after fielding some odd negative line-ups away from home he chose to start with FOUR strikers!? (Walters, Jerome, Fuller & Crouch). [A few days later he was asked about this break with Pulis-tradition in the form of: "Who are you, & what have you done with the real Tony Pulis?!"] But Stoke missed their chances, particularly Jerome, and when Tony brought on Kenwyne for Fuller, The Oatcake had a dig at the manager for being defensive, despite there still being 3 strikers on the pitch, with two over 6'5"! If Stoke had got a draw, it would have been fine, but Cisse scored in the very last minute to bring the house down. Tony was doubly disgusted; the following week's final fixture was against Owen Coyle's troubled Bolton, and Tony had a softer spot for him than Hughes. The 2-2 draw condemned Bolton – if Wanderers had won, they'd have sent QPR down instead. [Hughes' QPR were playing in a famous game at the Etihad that day.]

The draw left Stoke in 14th position, tolerable but poor, and the start of the comedown feeling from the highs of the previous 14 months.

Valencia and the comedown

Stoke's reward for qualification from the Europa League group stage had been a glamorous encounter with Spanish legends Valencia, who had dropped down from the Champions League. Up until this fixture

Tony's preparation and commitment to the competition, particularly the tricky away ties, had rarely been in doubt. Winning 1-0 away in Split and Thun, 2-1 in Tel Aviv, and drawing 1-1 in Kiev were extraordinary results for a Europa novice and made great viewing for dedicated travelling Stoke fans (and those watching avidly at home on TV). Even a 1-3 defeat in Besiktas, bearing in mind that Stoke had already qualified, was still seen as an achievement; Fuller's awesome long-range strike (his last goal for the club) had seemingly put Stoke on the road to victory...before Upson got red-carded.

La media inglesa @LaMedi... 23 Feb 12
Bueno, el Stoke se quedó fuera tras perder 1-0 en **Valencia**. Y ni siquiera debutó **Lucas Dawson**. Vaya drama.

Lucas Dawson, the instantly recognisable unused sub for the Valencia game.

Stoke's home ties at The Brit were even more of a treat with 4 wins and a draw – Split (1-0), Thun (4-1), Besiktas (2-1), Tel Aviv (3-0), and Kiev (1-1) – a far superior record compared to Premier League royalty like Harry Redknapp's Top-3 side Spurs.

But Tony's preparation for the Valencia tie was disrupted by concerns in the Premier. Stoke lost 4 games in a row, including a 1-2 defeat to West Brom (at home!), which was enough to disturb anyone. Stoke dropped from the relative safety of 8th spot to a vulnerable 14th.

Tony still fielded a strong side in the home leg against the Spanish side, but the team went down 0-1, only beaten by a cracking strike by Topal. By the time of the second leg Tony had a difficult decision to make: try to overturn the Spaniards at the legendary Estadio Mestalla stadium or save his squad for the crucial back-to-back unglamorous home games against Swansea and Norwich.

With tough games with Chelsea, Liverpool, Spurs, Man City and Arsenal lined up afterwards, Tony felt that he needed the points more than he needed a Europa scrap. Decision made: Premier League survival came first.

Several thousands Stoke fans travelled to Valencia. Most of the other Europa away ties had been too difficult to negotiate, but a short trip to the Spanish Riviera was too good to miss. With the sun, the beer and the football, a good time was to be had by all. Even Tony's chosen team couldn't dim their day-in-the-sun, although it did astound them all. Only 3 players remained from the first leg (equally only 3 remained from their last league game), and NONE of the 11 started the next league game. In fact, four of the players who started that night (Collins, Woodgate, Arismendi and Diao) never played for Stoke ever again! Moreover, even though the club were entitled to 7 substitutes, Tony only took 4 including the youth/reserve captain, Kidsgrove's-own Lucas Dawson, who many Stoke fans struggling to even recognise.

Intriguingly, Villa manager Martin O'Neil had pulled the exact same stunt 3 years earlier. After drawing 1-1 with CSKA Moscow, he then took a drastically weakened team to Russia, losing 0-2. Travelling fans (without the sun and the beer) were understandably apoplectic, but he sited the home game with Stoke the following Sunday as vital with Villa in a 4th place Champions League spot. Unfortunately, this was the game Stoke came back to gain a 2-2 draw in the last few seconds, and his supporters never forgave him. Villa lost the next 4 games to top sides (Liverpool, Spurs, Man City, Man Utd), crashed out of a Champions League spot, and went out of the following season's Europa League in a qualifying round. O'Neill only lasted another season. Would Tony suffer the same fate?

In the event the Stoke team put up a heroic effort in Valencia's intimidating stadium, with Potters fans having a whale of a time cheering on their side with many a rendition of "Delilah". Even Valencia's only goal after 23 minutes didn't dampen their spirits as Stoke went out 0-2 on aggregate.

Thankfully for Tony Stoke won their next two league games, Swansea by 2-0 and Norwich by 1-0, easing any relegation worries, with the headlines screaming that "TP gets it right" when it came to his team selections. But many supporters reckoned he'd over-egged the 40-point - target pudding. What one side saw as shrewd management, the other side saw as Tony just-about-getting-away-with-it. The cup of goodwill was running dry.

Part 2 - The Last Hurrah

After playing 48 games in the 2010/11 Cup Final season, and playing 56 games in the 2011/12 Europa season, the 2012/13 season – Stoke's 150th Anniversary – was always going to be a let-down (and only 42 games).

The large squad, which had swelled to cope with the Europa and cup fixtures, was further enhanced by Stephen N'Zonzi (£3m from Blackburn), Charlie Adam (c£4m from Liverpool), Geoff Cameron (c£2m from the colonies), and at the last minute superstar Michael Owen (from Hello! magazine). These were a different class of player, clearly brought in to address the call for improvements in Stoke's playing style.

Tony stands alone during the League Cup defeat to Di Canio's Swindon

Unfortunately, they were also joined by Maurice Edu (£4m), Brek Shea (£2.5m) and Michael Kightly (£3m). Shockingly, Edu and Shea made only 4 appearances between them, whilst winger Kightly never came out from the shadow of Pennant or Etherington. It now seemed that Tony was behaving too much like a Premier League manager, and his judgement was called into question.

He wasn't the only one. Down at Loftus Road, Mark Hughes and QPR were spending a similar fortune with little to show for it. He even re-signed the much-maligned Kieron Dyer – he obviously hadn't received the warning tweet from The Oatcake! But following 12 games without a win to start the season, and just after a 0-1 defeat by Stoke, Hughes was sacked. He was replaced by Harry Redknapp who spent another obscene amount of money in the January window, but was still relegated. It was hard to criticise Tony when others were falling so flat on their faces.

Despite no wins in their first 6 games, drawing 1-1 with champions

Manchester City and 0-0 with Arsenal were seen as tolerable. Even defeat by an Ashley Cole late-winner at Stamford Bridge was credible.

But it was the home defeat by Swindon in the League Cup that was to play such a major part in Tony Pulis' downfall.

Although Tony had made several changes for this game, the line-up was still made up of credible first team players (with the possible exception of fading Matthew Upson). With Stoke trailing 1-2, Tony threw on heavyweights Peter Crouch and John Walters late-on, but The Potters crashed out to Paolo Di Canio's side by 3-4 in extra time. "We played seven or eight players who were playing their first or second game of the season really," he admitted. "But the game was won by the better team. Swindon were just better than us."

It was a crushing blow for Tony. With a large squad he needed extra cup-run fixtures to maintain his squad's match-fitness. Drawing Manchester City in the FA Cup 4th Round later in the season only compounded the problem (Stoke went down 1-0 to a late Zabaleta strike). Keeping all his players happy, particularly those on the fringes, was going to prove more difficult in a season with 14 games less than the previous season. Opportunities for the likes of Michael Owen proved noticeably scarce.

On the positive side, N'Zonzi was proving a hugely influential and exciting central player. Here was a midfielder who wanted the ball continuously, and always seemed to know what to do with it. What on Earth was he doing in a Tony Pulis team?! Was this an example of Tony's plan to push on to a more attractive style of play? Unfortunately, N'Zonzi seemed to occupy an area Charlie Adam would also excel in, so Tony stubbornly pushed Adam forward in a number of awkward looking positions, with only (and frustratingly) limited success. But at least it showed intent to shake things up: "I think bringing N'Zonzi and Charlie into the team, we look a little more fluid through the midfield."

What people were unaware of was a personal tragedy in Tony's private life, which he was able to keep out of the public eye. During the summer his first grandchild, Olivia, had died only two-weeks old. Their story only became public the following year when they were able to raise thousands for the charity Bliss to help care for premature and sick babies. It was an emotional time for the Pulis family, and it was tough for Tony to continue on as before as if everything was normal. "I really started to feel a bit empty, and I think I lost a bit of what I'm all about. I allowed things to go on at the football club I wouldn't normally."

The Last Run

Slowly, Stoke began carving out a decent set of results. In the weeks up to New Year, they went on an astonishing 10 match unbeaten run. It included coming from behind to beat Newcastle late on by 2-1, with great goals from John Walters and super-sub Cameron Jerome; another away win at West Brom (1-0); holding Spurs at White Hart Lane; and Charlie

Adam's goals seeing off QPR and Fulham (both 1-0). Even watching Stoke away wasn't such an ordeal: "I actually think we've played better this year away from home than what we have at home!" Tony claimed in November.

But the cherry on top for the 10 match run, and the best game of the season, was a 3-1 defeat of Liverpool on Boxing Day evening. There were three goals in the first 12 minutes; Suarez won a

Tony looking less than pleased talking to the BBC

penalty scored by Gerrard, Walters equalised, and Kenwyne Jones headed Stoke ahead for 2-1. It wasn't until the second half that Walters finished them off with a volley from a long-throw, but the whole thing was priceless. Stoke's performance was one of their finest; they didn't just beat the mighty Liverpool, they humiliated them.

The best goal of the season then came next in the last game in the run of 10, a 3-3 draw against Southampton. With Stoke down to 10 men, super-sub Jerome hit a crackerjack volley equaliser in the last minute that flew in off the underside of the bar. Despite only securing a draw, it brought the house down at The Brit.

It was surely going to be an exciting second half to the season.

Down the dustpipe

The 2012/13 season could have been Stoke's best ever Premier League season. After the Southampton game, Stoke were comfortably perched in 8th spot after producing a set of great results and performances, and were even putting some decent goals away. But the season suddenly turned on its axis. Goals of any sort became a rarity in the New Year, with only 1 win in 14 games. After just scraping past a struggling Reading team by 2-1, Stoke lost 6 out of 7 games and only managed 2 goals. Stoke slumped down the league and looked seriously rife for relegation.

Worse was Tony's inability to exploit the January transfer window. Desperate to bring in a couple of players, Tony's top-heavy squad looked fragile in (of all places) defence, where Marc Wilson – described by Tony as the best left back in the Premier – broke his leg, whilst Robert Huth was suspended. Instead, the club released Matthew Upson. Clearly not

happy about how the window had gone, Tony glossed over it and ploughed on. "The important thing is not to worry about what went on and what didn't go on…Whether it was my fault or somebody else's fault, I don't want to go into that," he stated, refusing to be drawn further.

Tony's career at Stoke had reached a

Michael Owen, a little surprised to find himself in Stoke

tipping-point. Although he had always had detractors in the crowd, it was now the supporters who had been loyal for so long who were becoming more vocal about the football they were watching, and it was starting to hurt the club. Despite prices being frozen for the sixth year running, early-bird season-ticket sales dipped noticeably when they went on sale in February 2013. This understandably rattled the cage of Stoke's CEO Tony Scholes, whom the manager was reported as having a "fractious" relationship with.

With a number of markers now pointing against the manager, the media camped outside as Tony came under intense pressure, whilst bemused fans couldn't see where the next goal was coming from, let alone the next point. Within the space of a few weeks, the perception of Tony's Stoke side changed from a credible Top-10 team, to a bunch of rabbits in the headlights, and the knives started to come out. It looked like rabbit stew was back on the menu.

It certainly wasn't a good time to have a newspaper quoting chief-scout and long-time side-kick Lindsay Parsons seemingly dissing Tony for not signing many of his recommendations, such as Demba Ba, Ben Arfa and Adebayor. As it was, the players were either injured, not available or way too expensive. Tony laughed it off: "I don't surround myself with 'yes' men. I'd rather have people who say what they think." However, even he must have been alarmed when Stoke subsequently dismissed Parsons.

With Tony under pressure to improve Stoke's playing style, it was also bad timing that his main protagonists began to fail him. N'Zonzi's skills began to freeze up in the winter weather. His season began to fall apart after his unlucky dismissal against Southampton for supposedly stamping (the red card was later rescinded after video evidence), but his retaliation in the Fulham game after his nose was broken was shocking, although he escaped a ban. Robert Huth wasn't so lucky in the same game, and an off-the-ball incident earned him a retrospective 3 match ban. John Walters was in the wars, often seen with a bandage round his head. Worse still, Peter Crouch understandably lost his goal-scoring touch after having several teeth kicked out in a game against Newcastle, for which he needed corrective surgery. Even the clearly frustrated Michael Owen rarely featured. The only good news was that finally Tony had found a role for Charlie Adam in midfield, and his bullish performances were slowly coming on-tap.

But Tony was clearly unhappy with the situation: "The big disappointment is that we lost Robert and Matty, and also Willo [Wilson] for a long period. The balance of the team hasn't been as good as it's been in previous years. We've tried to address that, but unfortunately we've fallen short. And whether that's my fault or somebody else's fault, I don't want to go into that!"

Thankfully, back-to-back wins at Harry's sinking QPR (2-0) and home to Norwich (1-0) rescued Stoke to Tony's safe 40 points. But there was no getting away from the fact that although it could and should have been seen as a transitional season after their Europa League adventures, overall it was deemed to be a huge disappointment as a result of the catastrophic New Year collapse.

The 2012/13 season showed up just how good and how bad Stoke could be under Tony Pulis. For example, 13th place may not have been his coveted top-half finish, but it meant that Stoke had finished in the Top-14 in the whole country five seasons in a row for the first time since the 1890s...when there had only been 14 clubs in the league anyway!

However, only 21 goals scored at home was dire; only Stoke's relegation seasons of 1990, 1985 and 1890 had been worse! Despite fans becoming more vocal on what they wanted to see in the way of entertainment, Pulis had continued to produce the rabbit from the hat in that predictable style of his.

Even Spurs (with the help of the referee) dampened the 150th Anniversary celebrations in the season's final home game, with Adam sent off and Stoke defeated by 1-2. What would be Tony's final game managing Stoke resulted in a 1-1 draw at Southampton, where he famously brought on Michael Owen for his last ever game, finishing the match with 3 strikers almost in the hope of going out with a win.

Two days later he was sacked by Stoke. Again.

Why he had to go...

When Tony left the club 'by mutual agreement with immediate affect' many were still caught by surprise, but it was generally felt to be inevitable. Tony had always known it was on the cards – he'd effectively cleared out his local Wychwood Park house in preparation – but must have wondered what more the club expected under the circumstances. There was every evidence that the following season would have been an improvement, but would that have been enough for all concerned? Consensus said no.

An article produced just before Tony's demise made the observation that the Stoke board had a reputation of standing by their previous heroic managers, Tom

Tony as youth coach at Rovers

Mather, Tony Waddington and Lou Macari when they went through some very thorny patches. As a result they had delivered promotions, stability, great football, great players, profits and even trophies. But times had clearly changed. That wasn't how things were done now.

One argument was that he failed to exploit/embrace/enthuse about Stoke's new youth Academy ambitions. Their idea was to capture and develop all the local young talent, rather than to buy in players developed by other academies. However, if this was a cause for dismissal, it would have been as laughable as the "failing to exploit the foreign transfer market" reason put forward when Tony was first sacked in 2005. He did bring through a few young players such as Andy Wilkinson and Ryan Shotton. He also pinched a spindly "still-growing" 19-year-old Ryan Shawcross for a song from under the nose of Alex Ferguson and developed him into one of the finest and most valuable defenders in the game. "If you have a look at the size of him now, it takes about 15-20 minutes for those legs to get going!"

He always claimed that finding more local stars was a major objective: "We have to produce more local players. We have to get the best players from Stoke-on-Trent." These were not the words of someone resistant to the club's plans. But he was naturally resistant to suggestions that Stoke's squad should be flooded with cheap academy players in the same way that the club had attempted to flood the squad with cheap Icelandic players. And he was certainly indignant to

By the end, Tony needed a good ironing

suggestions that he didn't give youth a chance: "Sometimes it gets lost in the wash. Everybody wants to have a young vibrant team, everybody wants young players but they have to be good enough."

Another argument went that his face and his playing style did not fit the new global football market, as the Far East and North America began to pour in billions in revenue. The idea that the world was going to see The Britannia Stadium only three-quarters full of grumbling fans was unacceptable, not because of lost season-ticket revenue (a mere drop in the ocean) but because of losing prestige (and subsequent revenue) to the watching world.

This particularly applied to Pulisball, a style of football they were (rather unfairly) gaining a reputation for. However, much the supporters played up to it – "We'll Play How We Want!" and "1-0 to the Rugby Team!" – it was a reputation that stuck and needed addressing.

Unfortunately, Tony also played on it, trying to intimidate opponents by emphasising an over-exaggerated physical approach: "Psychologically, maybe to my detriment at times, I would actually build that up," he would later admit. Even when it was pointed out to him that in fact The Emirates had witnessed the highest number of free-kick goals rather than The Brit, he quipped: "Well, it's the way Wenger plays!"

It was felt that Tony had been given his opportunity in that final season to "push on" style-wise, and for whatever reasons hadn't delivered. To an established Premier side, the manager said more about the club than cash ever could, and a new face for the new 'marque' was required.

But what made certain Stoke executives uncomfortable was that Tony controlled so much off-the-field "infrastructure", as even he started to refer to it. His influence over coaches, scouts, directors, plus Director Of Football and Chairman was unprecedented. In fact, when Tony left, half the staff left too! Most were pushed, but some jumped.

However, he had every justification to have such a close-knit back-room team as this was what brought much of the stability for success. Arguably, Stoke stayed up in 2012-13 because of it; without it the club might easily have imploded and gone down. No Premier club allows that sort of power now. The power bases enjoyed by Tony or the likes of Alex Ferguson are probably gone forever. Clubs feel they need control at this level, and Tony held too many markers. His successor would hold no such power, allowing the club executives to make decisions concerning anything from the everyday running of the club to promoting themselves in the American and Asian markets in any way they saw fit.

In many ways Tony was a victim of his own success. He'd done his bit, now it was time to pass the baton. To many it seemed very cruel, and to a large number of non-Stoke fans there was genuine bewilderment and sympathy. As one fan tweeted, he could leave the club with his head held high...just like his players.

But it was done. On the Sunday he'd gained a point for Stoke at St Mary's. On Monday he'd undertaken a pre-arranged coaching course in Cardiff. And on Tuesday 21st May 2013 he'd driven all the way up from Poole to the Etruria offices of bet365 to meet Peter and John Coates, only to be told on entering the room that he was not being kept on. It could have been worse: they could have taken the car off him and told him to get the bus home.

It may have hurt, but it was a hell of a lot better than his split with Gillingham.

Chapter 8 – Resurrection! (2013-)

Part 1 – Tony Pulis, The Wilderness ~~Years~~ Days

Of course, it was generally felt that after leaving Stoke, Tony Pulis would spend the rest of his days in an old deck-chair on Branksome Beach, wearing his old baggy jogging bottoms, with strands of straggly hair protruding from the back of a tatty old baseball cap. Of course, this was only 'generally felt' by wistful Port Vale supporters and certain Gillingham executives. Tony had other ideas.

Raising money for charity involved Tony hanging out with some dubious characters...

After spending time with his family in Florida, he decided to take in the sights: "I went to the Crimea and spent a week looking at different things. I saw the field where the charge of the Light Brigade took place. I saw the palace where Churchill and Roosevelt divided the world up after the war." It turned out not to be the only palace he would see in 2013.

It was strange time for him, a time of the year when he would normally be religiously preparing for pre-season training, and doing the ground work for late August transfer signings. He didn't even get a call from Boston United!

It would certainly give him more time to be involved in his ambitious and occasionally dangerous charity projects. Whereas some people grew beards to raise funds, Tony would always try something a bit more strenuous. In recent years he had followed a London Marathon run with a 1000 mile bike-ride from John O'Groats to Lands End with comedian Nick Hancock. He even got to carry the Olympic torch (as a late stand-in for athlete Emma Jackson). But he may have overreached himself with his plan to ascend Mount Kilimanjaro, where many of the party had to be helped off the mountain suffering from altitude sickness and hypothermia, as temperatures dropped alarmingly to -33°. Tony described the whole experience as "a nightmare". "At times it was really scary, but the main thing was we made it. All in all, it was the toughest physical challenge of my life!" Up ahead lay experiences that were far less perilous, but still thorny in nature.

As the 2013/14 season began, he was soon back in front of the cameras, only this time working with the media. He somehow looked like he felt he should be somewhere else, but couldn't quite think where. One of his first jobs was with the new BT Sports channel and their first ever live Premier game; and, yes, it just had to be Liverpool vs Stoke City.

From the word go everyone was wanting him to twist the knife on Stoke, the Coates family and CEO Tony Scholes, but to his credit he continued to show great loyalty. He stuck to his original official statement which had said:

"I have enjoyed some wonderful times at Stoke City and nobody was prouder than me when, after 23 years of exile from top-flight football, we gained Barclays Premier League status.

"Of course, having reached the top you then have to find a way to stay there and develop a strategy for a Club that had no infrastructure in place to compete with the top Championship clubs we had left behind, never mind the top Premier League clubs.

"Peter, his family and I have enjoyed every inch of the journey; he has been truly a fantastic man to work with. Although I am disappointed, I do understand what he means when he says the Board feels a need to take the Club in a different direction.

"In leaving I am very proud of what we have all achieved. My immediate staff lead (sic) by David Kemp, my backroom staff and all the training ground staff have been absolutely wonderful."

In a personal message to Stoke fans who'd contacted him, he concluded: "I wish you good luck and over 40 points for next season and for the foreseeable future."

Despite a vast increase in passing (50%) and a vast decrease in long-balls (-30%), Stoke lost that first game by 0-1, after his favourite Jon Walters had missed a late penalty. It did not go unnoticed (not just by BT) that in his 5 Premier League games at Anfield Tony's Stoke had managed three draws. Tony may not have been drawn on the changing style of play (albeit still very much in its infancy), but Stoke fans certainly were, as they out-sang The Kop with "We're Stoke City, we're passing the ball!"

Spot the Pulisball

By August, Pulis-spotting was becoming an epidemic, as were the rumours that came with them. He was seen back in the dugout chatting to Harry Redknapp, but only as part of some media duties for BBC's Radio5Live for a QPR cup game. He was soon linked with Sunderland when Paolo Di Canio dropped off the radar. He was then spotted at a

match chatting to the CEO of Derby County, who had just sacked Nigel Clough. He was then linked with Middlesbrough, who had just parted with Tony Mowbray. It was even suggested that Southampton might be an ideal fit (being so close to home), but instead of struggling under Mauricio Pochettino The Saints had a brilliant start to the season (tellingly, Pochettino would later jump ship at the end of the season after they'd finished 8th). On and on it went.

Harry Redknapp looking suitably startled

After a time, it did look like he was either determined to stay out of management, or just looking for an offer he couldn't refuse. One offer he would have struggled to turn down was the Wales job. Under-fire national manager Chris Coleman looked certain to be let go after a string of poor results, particularly as his contract was allowed to run out without a new one being offered. Change was surely afoot. He was even being touted to return to Crystal Palace where he had been a player. Instead, the Welsh FA weighed up the alternatives and finally offered him a two year extension on his contract on 14th November 2013; so that avenue for Tony was closed.

Tony's footballing reputation ran ahead of him so much that clubs and fans openly ruled him out before a vacancy even appeared. It was questioned as to whether any Premier League club would employ him. And although he showed his willingness to drop a division, many Championship sides were equally coy.

Of course, a struggling Premier club looking for an impact manager could always be relied on to appear as if from nowhere, and sure enough one turned up. On the 23rd October 2013, Tony's old friend and Bristol Rovers colleague Ian Holloway fell on his sword at Crystal Palace, leaving them 2nd from bottom (they were propped up by Sunderland who'd just appointed Gus Poyet), but already 5 points from relegation safety. Their record for the season was 8 defeats and one win (naturally against Sunderland by 3-1). Palace were careering out of control, odds on to do-a-Derby.

After gaining promotion and then losing star winger Wilfried Zaha to Manchester United in the summer for £10m, "Ollie" Holloway had brought in SIXTEEN new players, which turned out to be too many too quickly, and the club leaked goals like a sieve. "We need to shut up shop in this division," Ollie admitted, ruefully. "I have to hold my hand up and say we didn't keep the spirit that got us up. We changed too much too quickly." His co-chairman Steve Parish concurred: "We've got a whole group of people who are only really used to the Championship and dropped them into the Premier League. I think we both realised we need someone with more experience at this level."

Naturally enough, Tony Pulis's name came up immediately, but his response was non-committal. "It was important to take a rest. I'm really pleased I've had contact from other clubs but they didn't feel right." In fact, he didn't show much interest at all, no doubt more interested at the time to see how the Wales situation panned out.

SUN SOCCER CARD No 846

D. KEMP (Carlisle United)

Dave Kemp wondering what life would bring him
© *News Group Newspapers*

Apart from the fact that it seemed like everyone he'd ever been associated with had managed them (Neil Warnock, George Burley, Ian Holloway, etc – even David Kemp and Gerry Francis had played there), Tony did have one important link with Palace. Taking over as caretaker-manager from Ollie was an ex-Palace apprentice called Keith Millen, who'd been a solid defender for Brentford and Watford. However, what many didn't realise was that in 1999 he'd been signed to Bristol City...by none-other-than Tony Pulis. Tony had even made him captain.

"I know Tony well," Millen said, when Tony's name came up for the Palace job. "He signed me as a player for Bristol City. He reminds me of Sam Allardyce in that he knows which teams to put out to win and not necessarily with the best group of players in the league. His biggest asset is that he knows how to win football matches in the Premier League. As for Tony's style of play," he added, "you win games, don't you?"

Whilst Tony considered his options, Millen had to deal with Arsenal at home and West Brom away, both 0-2 defeats. That meant Palace had lost SEVEN games in a row, 10 defeats out of 11 games in all. After a 0-0 draw with Everton, they were 3 points adrift at the bottom of the Premier, and 6 points from safety. They'd scored only 6 goals – the lowest in all 4 divisions – and conceded 21 – only Sunderland (22) had conceded more in the Premier.

One thing was certain: Tony didn't come cheap. It was reported that he commanded an annual salary at Stoke of circa £1.5m + bonuses, a trifle more than the average Potteries worker. He also had doubts as to whether the job of Premier League survival for the club was actually possible. So Palace co-chairman Steve Parish broadened his search to Chris Coleman (who ultimately stayed in Wales), Martin O'Neill (who abruptly took the Republic Of Ireland job a few days later), Dan Petrescu (whose compensation package to Dynamo Moscow was equally prohibitive), and even Iain Dowie (despite the bitter legal dispute with Palace when he'd been manager there several years before).

It wasn't so surprising then that Parish returned to Tony Pulis. With huge Premier League earnings estimated at circa £60m, he would be worth the investment. But Tony did need persuading:

"I met Steve the one time and I didn't feel as though it was right. Then he wanted to have a chat again. He came down to Bournemouth and we had a good chat about it, and he convinced me that it was a challenge. Looking at it, everyone I had spoken to had said it was a difficult one. Alex Ferguson and Peter Coates were the only two who said to take it. And they were two good judges. The rest were very negative towards it. I hadn't seen Palace play and what they had or didn't have. But I enjoy a challenge. It's in my nature to stand up and try to march people forward."

Of course, Alex Ferguson wasn't always able to judge managerial success – David Moyes at United being the most memorable – but he always seemed to have a soft spot for Tony: "I have a great admiration for Tony and the wry way he rides the criticism. If anything, it galvanises his players. People have criticised their physical style of play but they stick to what they do best. I suppose Arsene Wenger has been one of their main critics, but then he does go off on a tangent at times."

We're Getting The Band Back Together!

So a month to the day after Ollie had left, Tony was announced as the new manager of Crystal Palace on Saturday 23rd November 2013 with a two and half year contract. Soon, Dave Kemp and Gerry Francis were on board too – other gang members would no doubt have joined later. Unlike at Plymouth, where Tony had jumped in to start the job before a 2 week international break, he'd left it until the end of the break to take charge at Selhurst Park. However, just like at Stoke in 2002, the delay in appointment had seen more poor results, leaving Palace bottom of the league. Astonishingly, Stoke City were only 3 places above them in 17th spot! Maybe they would go down together, suggested some sceptical observers.

Bleeding Keith Millen making his debut for Bristol City against...Stoke

But Millen's approach had impressed Tony, and despite 2 defeats and a draw, Palace's performances particularly at league leaders Arsenal, were markedly improved. Keeping the season's first clean sheet in the Everton game was all the more to his liking. So it was less of a surprise that Tony chose to watch his new side from the stand, leaving Millen in charge for the Hull away fixture on the day of his appointment. It paid dividends.

Palace tore into Hull, so much so that Palace striker Marouane Chamakh was soon injured in a clash of heads, resulting in Cameron Jerome (on loan from Stoke) coming on in the first half. Jerome, who'd fallen out of favour with Tony in the past, put on a dazzling display. But Steve Bruce's Hull were no pushovers, but a decent mid-table side who hadn't lost at home all season. However, they were now being dogged by a war between supporters and the owner over the changing of their name to Hull Tigers, which worked against them, particularly as Palace went down to 10 men on 78 minutes when Bolasie was unfortunate to be red-carded. Three minutes later, man-of-the-match Jerome beat his man and set up Barry Bannan to score the winner from close range. It was Palace's first goal for 434 minutes. Palace fans couldn't believe it, and joined in the myth by singing: "One Keith Millen, there's only one Keith Millen".

The win took the club off the bottom, immediately taking the steam out of what looked like a dire situation, and Tony was quick to acknowledge the fact: "I am very happy to be at the club and this result makes it a great start for me. The first thing I'd like to do is thank Keith for what he has done over the last few weeks. Personally, it is triffic for me to come in on the back of a win." Despite Kempy being in the wings, Tony wisely made Millen his assistant-manager.

Preparation started in haste for Tony's first proper game in charge this time at Norwich, two places above Palace. He knew he had inherited a good squad from Ian Holloway, in the same way that Ollie had inherited a good squad at Plymouth from Tony. But it would take time to get the results however fast he tried to move things: "We have a great spirit within the group. They've trained really well. What we've done on the pitch has been really difficult for them. If there's a criticism, most probably, it's that I've tried to put too much into them too quickly. But their attitude has been absolutely first class."

After the Hull victory, fans were more receptive to life under Tony Pulis. He may not have been their No.1 choice, but he did have a certain reputation: to reverse failing fortunes.

For the Norwich game he recalled on-loan-players Jerome and Jason Puncheon for their first starts since Ollie had left. Although Palace went down to a single goal, sending them bottom again, there were clear signs of resurrection, with 13 shots to Norwich's 10. But Tony didn't have to wait long for the next game, his first home game in charge.

The Clash Of The Chubby Browns

Three days later, Palace took on Sam Allardyce's West Ham, with the game being billed as a "clash-of-the-longball-titans" and as "coarsely-unsubtle-as-a-Roy-Chubby-Brown-DVD". Tony had beefed up Palace's defence, and with the likes of Puncheon seemingly reborn, The Eagles took the lead just before half-time with a Chamakh glancing header, a goal that rankled Big Sam – the striker had failed to score when on loan to The Hammers the previous season. Palace then fought the standard Tony Pulis tooth-and-nail way to keep the lead for their 1-0 victory, allowing them to leapfrog Sunderland again in the table.

Purists pointed at the typically low 37% possession-rate for a Tony Pulis game, certainly compared to Ollie's figures – Palace's only other win that season was a 3-1 victory over Sunderland where possession was 48%. However, it was also pointed out that Palace's previous home game, the hard-fought 0-0 with high-flying Everton, resulted in a staggeringly low 27% possession-rate. But in the next match – a 2-0 victory over Cardiff, fuelled by Jerome and Chamakh goals – possession was a colossal 44%! Journalists scratched their heads – stats clearly proved nothing.

With Palace beginning to draw level with teams in safe positions, Tony was delighted with his players, chucking out sound-bites like there was no tomorrow: "Back to back wins doesn't half give a club a lift." "You've always got a chance if you get yourself

Tony doing the laundry at Palace before his first game in charge

organised." "We can't get carried away. Staying up is a massive ask and a massive task."

The "massive task" was made more difficult by 2 defeats, although Palace came close to a point at Chelsea. They went down with a fight by 1-2, at a ground where Tony had come close to causing an upset on a number of occasions (well, except possibly for the 0-7 defeat four years before). A 1-3 home defeat to a Newcastle side chasing a Europa spot was more worrying. It was one of the poorest Palace performances of the season, and showed the fragility of the side.

But a Boxing Day robbery at poor old Aston Villa, mugged yet again in the last seconds by a Pulis-side, saw the club move out of relegation with a stonking Dwight Gayle solo effort. Before the game Tony had revealed his concerns about a player whom Ollie had paid a whopping

£6m for a few months before. "I think it is a very big ask to get a kid who was playing non-league football only a year ago to go and play straight in the Premier League. When I first came to the club Dwight was the marquee signing. We'd spent a lot of money on him and it looked like he

Tony watches in horror

had the weight of the world on his shoulders in lots of respects. He wasn't really integrated, so we spent a lot of time opening him up as a person and a player." But he did have some sympathy for the seemingly overlooked Gayle, who'd come on late as sub for Jerome: "I'm a manager that picks a team and, if you're in that team, it's more difficult to get out of the team, that's the way I've always managed." More scratching of heads for journos, but Gayle at least must have got the gist.

As for Palace's low scoring record so far, Tony added: "I am not worried about that. If we score one goal and the opposition score none, then we get three points. It makes no difference to me."

Only two days later, Palace players put up a sterling performance at Manchester City's Etihad Stadium, a place that Tony lost regularly and meekly and usually by 0-3 (well, 4 seasons out of 5). This time, despite City averaging 4 goals a game at home, Palace matched them shot-for-shot, and only went down to a Edin Dzeko strike which sent City top for the first time, putting the millionaires on the road to the Premier League Championship.

Unfortunately, this was followed by a rain-soaked home draw with Norwich (1-1) and the defeat at Spurs (0-2) where Puncheon sliced an early penalty off in the direction of Dagenham (somewhere the other side of the corner flag).

This was Palace's unsatisfying preparation for Tony's biggest game of the season in mid-January 2014.

Meanwhile Back At The Farm...Again

The idea behind Tony's departure from Stoke was that City were going in a "different direction". But what exactly did that mean?

Months before Tony had left the club in 2013, chairman Peter Coates was talking about Stoke being "self-sufficient" as early as 2014. However, most of this would be achieved with the massive increases in Premier League TV income that were just over the horizon. Obviously this relied on Stoke remaining in the Premier, and not overspending in the transfer market. It also depended on control of the increasing wage bill of £50m, which although massive, was still only the 15th highest of the 20 Premier clubs.

A week after Tony and his gang were evicted, The Potters appointed Mark Hughes on May 30th

Sparky arriving to play a fund-raiser for Tony's struggling Gillingham side in July 1995

2013. Hughes' brief was to keep costs down (particularly those transfer fees), exploit the academy, play attractive football, and get Stoke into the top half of the Premier League and keep them there. Silverware would be useful too. It was quite a task.

On the face of it, Hughes seemed the LAST person for the job. As even he would later admit, "I came under difficult circumstances. My star had faded somewhat, so the Coates family placed a lot of faith in my ability." Hughes had been encouraged to spend wildly in his previous job at Queens Park Rangers, only to start the 2012/13 season with a string of dreadful results, including an opening day 0-5 defeat at home to Swansea. Even before his QPR played Stoke in November, broadcaster George Andrews pertinently summed up Hughes' player strategy as "looking as if he's just put them in a bag and thrown them on the pitch." A Charlie Adam strike subsequently sent Rangers back to the bottom of the league. A week later, QPR sacked Hughes with the club on course for relegation, for which chairman Tony Fernandes never forgave him. Even Harry Redknapp couldn't save them.

Peter Coates described Hughes' QPR experience as a "blip", stating that he had a good record elsewhere. This was true to a certain extent.

He had indeed been prudent in the mid-2000s with Blackburn, and when he had started spending there more lavishly, he brought in quality players (whom Rovers cashed in after he left).

But at the same time that Tony gave up his prudency and blew £22m after promotion in 2008, Hughes was spending a colossal £128m in his

new job at Manchester City. It may have been his brief at the time, but it should have taught Hughes that money didn't buy success. Man City finished a disastrous 10th, only two places above Stoke City. The following season he

Many fans wanted Tony out, …but for Hughes?
(driver shown in silhouette only)

spent £118m at the start of the season, over £100m more than Stoke, and yet were only a few places higher. For Hughes, it was all over by Christmas.

He followed this with a decent season at Fulham, but left them as they appeared to lack ambition. More recently he explained further: "When I was there I had a few doubts over what kind of investment would be made available to strengthen the team. I interpreted that as maybe the club didn't want to keep on progressing. Almost immediately after I left they started investing in good players and spending some money, so I probably got that wrong."

So naturally the first question incredulous Stoke fans wanted to ask was, what the hell did Mark Hughes bring to the party that Tony Pulis didn't offer? They were willing to accept Tony's departure as inevitable, but replacing him with Mark Hughes didn't seem to make a lot of sense. The situation was epitomised by a guy named Carl driving round the city with "HUGHES OUT" displayed in big letters on his van.

But Hughes talked the talk at his first press conference, was keen to follow the club's new direction, and soon fans could see progress on the pitch. He fully exploited Tony's former players, bringing out a new side to them, and his few signings were quality but measured. One of the few times he overstepped the mark was when he cheekily re-signing released Jermaine Pennant, an act that made him appear to be a thumbing his nose at Tony. Initially seen as a success (he won them all 3 points at

West Ham with a stunning free kick), it all turned sour again (he bizarrely cost them all 3 points against Everton), and Pennant was soon showed the door.

Initially Stoke's passing game looked absurd and contrived. Even Stoke defenders looked stressed as they fought the temptation to hoof the ball forward. But performances, particularly away from home where Tony's teams had struggled, were vastly improved, even if the results didn't match them. In fact, by mid-November when Tony was taking over at Palace, the club

The "Celts": Hughes and Pulis

looked like they might be drawn into a relegation battle – one place above the drop – particularly after losing 0-4 to Everton.

But judging by performances, it was only a matter of time that a big result would come Stoke's way, and it came in December when they finally (after 38 years) beat Chelsea in the league by 3-2 in a stunning game. Slowly but surely, the new Stoke City was appearing. Those monkeys were finally tumbling off their backs.

Pulis vs Hughes

Stoke's build up to their game at Selhurst Park was, however, the stuff of nightmares, even worse than Palace's. Stoke lost 1-5 at Newcastle, lost 0-3 at Spurs, frustratingly drew 1-1 at home to Everton (with Pennant inexplicably giving away a late penalty equaliser), and then conceded five again in a 3-5 defeat at home to Liverpool.

It still didn't change the fact that with Palace back at the foot of the table and Stoke hanging on to 12th spot, both sides needed to win the game. Although both managers appeared cool on the outside, they too both desperately wanted to win this game. Behind the scenes, Tony took every opportunity to remind his players of this, and his desire for his new club to match Stoke point-for-point.

For the fans it was an emotional rollercoaster. Many of the 2,500

Stoke fans came down with messages for their former manager, some in the form of banners showing their appreciation for Tony's work at Stoke. One read "Thank you, Tony – Always a Legend!" Another said "Changes are made, but memories NEVER fade. Thanks Tony." One, paraphrasing the immortal words of Gloria Gaynor, read "We Never Did Say Goodbye! Happy Birthday TP. Good Luck From All Stoke Fans". [The game was played on January 18th, 2 days after his 56th birthday.] Even Palace fans picking up on the emotions of the day, particularly when Tony came out to a rousing welcome from effectively the whole ground. Then the game started, and all sentimentality was put aside.

It wasn't a classic. Hughes put out a side with 9 Pulis-players, and amazingly had 57% possession, unheard of even in a Mark Hughes away game (they were struggling to get anywhere near that percentage at The Brit!). But a goal finally came after half-time as Stoke dithered in their own box, allowing Puncheon to score through Shawcross' legs. Tony's celebration was noticeably muted.

Crystal Palace – or Crystal Pulis as it had been re-christened by many – held on for the points. Stoke dropped to 13th, only 2 points ahead of Palace, who'd risen 4 places off the bottom. Palace even had a better away record than Stoke, who'd only won one and drawn 2. However, both sides were about to go on impressive runs, with Stoke convincingly beating Manchester United (2-1).

The 1-0 win against Stoke took Palace out of the relegation zone, and they had no intensions of going back. With the media predicting lavish spending from Tony in the January window, in the end he was relatively restrained. Puncheon was naturally signed permanently for £1.75m. He couldn't stop scoring, and was turning into a Selhurst hero. Two of Tony's long-time targets were finally landed; 6ft 5in defender Scott Dann, was brought in for £1.5m, and Joe Ledley was signed for a mere £700k. Goalkeeping cover was secured with Wayne Hennessey for £1.5m, particularly as the brilliant 34 year old Julian Speroni was out of contract in a few months time.

It was restrained compared to what Ollie had spent at the beginning of the season (nearly 4 times as much). What was interesting was that it was generally felt that all of these players would have cost Tony considerably more if he'd signed them for Stoke.

The Tony Pulis machine marched on with home wins against Hull (by 1-0, Puncheon again) and the poor unfortunate West Brom (3-1), with perhaps inevitable defeats at Arsenal (0-2) and home to Manchester United (0-2). But Tony realised he now had to pace his team, as the run-in included home games against Chelsea, Manchester City and Liverpool, and a set of tough away fixtures against relegation-seekers. So, when Palace lost at home to Southampton by 0-1 in March, and then couldn't overcome Sunderland (0-0) or Newcastle (0-1, with Tony grumbling about being "beaten by the last kick of the game" by Cisse), the vultures began to gather. With the club still hovering just outside the drop-zone, Tony needed 12 points from somewhere to reach his golden target of 40, but no one seemed sure where he would get any of these points from.

José and Brendan

Typically in these situations, Palace's next game was home to rampant Chelsea, whom Tony had only beaten once and that had been as a player 34 years previously – although in fairness it had started a riot. It would probably cause another riot if he could do it again – Chelsea were joint 2nd, and had battered Arsenal 6-0 the previous weekend. But amazingly with the help of a John Terry headed

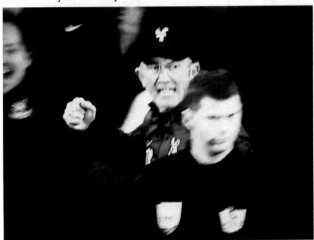

Tony showing traditional passion - linesmen beware!

own-goal, under-pressure from Joe Ledley, Palace did just that, in a remarkable victory taking them up to 16th. As Jose Mourinho put it "For their spirit, their commitment, their desire, they deserved it." It was like listening to Alan Hansen.

This was astonishing for the media. It had seemed an impossible enough job to get Palace off the bottom and then out of relegation, but to beat Chelsea seemed unbelievable. But they found that the best was yet to come. Palace followed it up with an inspired 3-0 win at Cardiff, with Ledley taking the plaudits again, this time on his return to his boyhood club. Next up was a 1-0 win (Puncheon yet again) against the desperate relegation-threatened Villa.

But a result away at Champions-League seeking Everton, who had just won SEVEN league games in a row, including Arsenal by 3-0, was surely out of the question. But Everton were unceremoniously flattened

by Palace in this re-arranged mid-week fixture. Puncheon took an opportunist's goal, and in the second half Dann headed home from a corner for 2-0. Everton pulled one back for 2-1, giving the crowd hope of a recovery, until Puncheon powered in to set up Jerome for 3-1, with a late Everton consolation to make the final score at Goodison 3-2 to Palace.

Beating Roberto Martinez's Everton was remarkable. Here Martinez curiously celebrates his first ever Wigan goal...in Tony's first league game as Gillingham manager.
The Gills came back to win 2-1

"Remarkable," said Tony, although it was hard to tell if he meant the game or the fact that the club had reached his precious 40 points and safety. "This is a different team to what I had at Stoke, with different strengths. I think we're an exciting team." And for once the football world even agreed.

But the best was STILL yet to come. After a 1-0 win at West Ham – the fourth club that Palace had done the double over that season, and their fifth win in a row – Palace faced Manchester City. The Sky Blues had slipped to 3rd, but could mount an assault on Liverpool who were 6 points ahead, particularly as The Reds had just been beaten 2-0 at Anfield by 2nd place Chelsea an hour before. This time Palace fell away to lose 0-2 at home, but there was a standard reason for this, believed Tony: "Playing against some teams, it's not a level playing field. We've been beaten by the most expensive club side in world sport. We now have to prepare ourselves for Liverpool." And prepare they did.

Brendan Rodgers was unimpressed. Not only had Tony Pulis won *his* Manager Of The Month award for April, but up until that weekend his Liverpool side had their destiny in their own hands. They really needed to beat Palace away and Newcastle at home in their last two games to stay level with Man City. The Palace vs Liverpool game was on the

Monday night after all the weekend games had been played. With Man City winning at Everton, it was all the more important for The Reds to bring back 3 points.

And things were on track for Rodgers as Liverpool roared ahead to a 3-0 lead within the hour. With an inferior goal-difference to Man City, The Reds foolishly pushed forward in the reasonable pursuit of a landslide. But the alarm bells should have started ringing when Damien

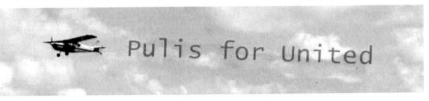

Wishful thinking on somebody's part...

Delaney blasted in from 25 yards, with 11 minutes left. They should have, but they didn't. As a result, super-sub Gayle scored two great goals in the last 10 minutes to make it 3-3, as Palace suddenly seemed to overwhelm them, and Liverpool fell apart. The Selhurst Park crowd went barmy. OK, it may not have been a win, but what a comeback, what a performance. As the final whistle went, Suarez and the like were in tears, but Palace players were jubilant as they celebrated their last home game of an extraordinary season. Sheer joy and bitter tears: That's how much this game meant to everyone.

Now the media really were astonished. They had been ready to crown Liverpool as Premier League champions for the very first time, and to award the Manager Of The Year to Rodgers. But now all that had changed. Everyone had been impressed by Tony Pulis' season at Palace, but this 3-3 draw against Liverpool was the most amazing moment of them all. Even Tony seemed a little startled as to where the comeback had come from, although there was a hint that it may have been inspired by his substitutions Gayle and Glenn Murray. "The two of them linked up really well. It was the right time to bring them on because the game had got a bit stretched. And when it's stretched, there's more space for Gayley." He even added, with a wry smile: "When we got the third goal, you're thinking we could go on and win it!"

Palace drew their last game at relegated Fulham by 2-2, to finish 11th, their third best finish ever, and only 2 places below Stoke, who'd also finished well, including defeats of Man Utd and Arsenal. Many did the arithmetic and worked out that if the season had started when Tony had joined Palace, then the league may have looked exactly the same at the top and bottom...but in the middle, Palace would have finished 8th (41 pts) with Stoke a point behind in 9th (40 pts). Above them in 7th place would have been Manchester United in 7th (44 pts), with many United fans observing that even Tony could have done a better job at Old Trafford than David Moyes!

Part 2 – 40 Years On

40 years in professional football is a pretty amazing achievement for anyone these days. But to reach your 40th year and have your career still rising exponentially is quite remarkable.

Who would have believed that the small gangly 16 year old signing for Rovers in 1974 would slowly but determinedly rise to be The Premier League's Manager Of The Season, with the Barclays trophy presented to him at a special awards dinner on 12th May 2014.

Tony won the award ahead of Brendan Rodgers (who won the LMA Manager Of The Year), Manuel Pellegrini (who won the Premier League), and Arsene Wenger (who won the FA Cup).

Suddenly he was on the same platform as previous winners such as Alex Ferguson, Jose Mourinho, Kenny Dalglish, Harry Redknapp,

WE ARE NO MORE THE YO-YO CLUB 'CPFC' THANK 'U' MR. PULIS

A banner at Selhurst Park. Fans enjoying "the ride" at Crystal Palace

Arsene Wenger, and, er, George Burley. [Burley had won it 18 months before he turned the Stoke job down, an act that had opened the door for Tony.]

Nobody was now going on about the fact that since he'd taken over Crystal Palace their possession rates had fallen to 35%, well below the other Premier teams. Instead the media were lamenting the end of Pulis-ball, raving that Crystal Pulis had the third fewest crosses from open play (only beaten by Liverpool and Chelsea).

Also, only a small fraction of Palace's goals had come from set-pieces compared to Pulis' time at Stoke.

For a manager renowned for teams hoofing the ball forward, it was particularly noted that the number of attempted long-balls were suitably restrained at Palace compared to his Premier League days at Stoke City. The only season it was less was Tony's final season at Stoke (2012/13), where the stats certainly showed his attempts to change the direction of play there.

But although Tony loves his stats, he often plays them down when he's asked about them:

"The biggest stat is that we've the lowest budget in the Premiership, and we've finished 11th. We've over-achieved at this football club massively. It's been fantastic – it's been a great ride!"

And although he's been at it for 40 years, he's still passionate about football and forever looking forward:

"Palace is a wonderful club, it's got fantastic potential. But it's so far behind in lots of respects. I did this at Stoke with Peter Coates, a wonderful chairman, we built it up over several years, and it will remain a Premier League football club for a generation. So we know how to do it. We need things put in place and the backing to do it."

The Crystal Maze

Unfortunately, it wouldn't be at Selhurst Park. On Thursday 14th August 2014, 2 days before the start of the new season, Tony split from Crystal Palace. He had struggled with plans to develop the club and to bring in key players with co-Chairman Steve Parish and sporting director Iain Moody. To do this he needed more control of club affairs than Parish would offer. For a serious, long-term position, Tony required a proper power-base. But chairmen understandably see managers today as transient, and are reluctant to allow managers to establish themselves and put down roots. It was the same old argument.

Not so for long-serving manager Arsene Wenger, who surprisingly backed-up Tony by saying: "The guy responsible for the results should be responsible for buying the players. Transfers should be the manager's job. If not, we are just robots."

It was obvious from the start that Tony was concerned that Palace couldn't offer what he needed to do the job, despite them all seeming to work so well together in that first season: "The great thing about Iain is he's signed the players I've wanted, not signing players without me knowing about them; and they were within a certain budget I had spoken to Steve Parish about." Even with statements like this, it always sounded like Tony was choosing his words carefully. It wasn't right, and in the end it just broke.

But Tony was always philosophical: "You have good experiences and bad experiences in life. The great thing for me is I wasn't a great player – I managed at the lower level and managed to be successful and that gives great hope to everyone else. For me to do what I've done, I'm very proud, but that was yesterday. I've got a long way to go, and I've got a lot of things I want to do in my life."

It doesn't sound like Tony Pulis is planning to retire quite yet. Whatever you might think of his teams, the man is a footballing treat wherever he goes and whatever he does. Predictable yet unpredictable, one minute he's climbing a mountain, the next he's stepping in to carry the Olympic Torch.

Love him or hate him, plan to be entertained by his presence for a good few years more.

That old deck-chair on Branksome Beach might have to wait a bit longer.

Anthony Richard Pulis
Based in Poole, Baked In Florida

Appendix - Tony Pulis' Iconic Games

Bristol City 1 Bristol Rovers 1 – Sat 30th Aug 1975, Att 17,918

It was the Welshman replacing the Scotsman as Tony Pulis made his debut in a number 8 shirt for Rovers in this Bristol derby, coming in for injured Glaswegian Tom Stanton. Whilst some colleagues were helpfully trying to keep youngsters like Tony calm before the game, others players – mainly local lads – earnestly reminded everyone that losing a derby meant making yourself scarce round town for a few days/weeks/months/years. Despite City being the promotion pushers, Rover took an early lead in the 3rd minute when Bruce Bannister connected with a free-kick, before Paul Cheesley headed City back on level-terms on 19 minutes. From then on the Rovers' keeper effectively kept them in it, until Tony had his 1-on-1 with the City keeper late in the game, which surely would have sealed it for The Pirates. Beating the offside-trap, Tony made it into the penalty area before lobbing it wide of the keeper and the goal. "I thought I had plenty of time.

Outside of the boot - textbook stuff

Then all of a sudden the keeper was on top of me. He came out so quickly that I had to hurry my shot and I put it wide." City went on to finish 2nd and were promoted to the top-flight, but tough-talking Rovers' manager Don Megson was still disappointed that his side didn't steal a win at Ashton Gate: "I must be honest and say that in no way was I pleased with our performance in the game. We did not play at all well. We introduced yet another young player, Tony Pulis, into the side. Because the team performance was not a good one he was not able to give the debut display I would have liked. But he did not let me down." Blimey, you just can't please some people.

Sunderland 0 Bristol Rovers 1 – Sat 07th Jan 1978, Att 26,214

For many years this FA Cup 3rd round win was Tony's most memorable game. He'd just taken over the No.8 Rovers shirt from his friend David Williams a few days before for the thrilling 3-2 "6-pointer" against Cardiff (last minute winner, coming from behind). Rovers had just parted company with manager Don Megson (off to the colonies) after a poor start to the season, only 3 wins in a 3 month period that included the catastrophic 0-9 annihilation at Spurs & the 1-5 humiliation

Shaun Penny finishes Tony's "goal"

at Sunderland, dragging Rovers into the relegation zone. His successor Bobby Campbell had managed 3 wins in 3 weeks as caretaker, so was given the full-time job just before this cup game. Understandably, Rovers hadn't won away all season. To make matters worse, they'd been drawn away from home in the FA Cup for a record TENTH time in a row. But amazingly, before Rovers

went down to 10 men, Bobby Gould connected with a 21st minute free-kick to lob in the only goal of the game. It was enough to secure a famous win for Tony's side in front of a large crowd at Roker Park. Campbell acknowledged that heroic defending against the Sunderland onslaught was what won it. "Even then," he added, "we were still geared to break forward when the pressure let up and with a bit of luck, we could have scored two more goals in the second half." Really? He was dreaming. Tony kept his place, and Rovers heroically beat Southampton 2-0 in the next round.

Bristol Rovers 3 Chelsea 0 – Sat 23rd Feb 1980, Att 14,176

Two years later and Bobby Gould, the Rovers hero of the Sunderland game, had become assistant manager at Chelsea under none-other-than Geoff Hurst. Chelsea had been relegated with Danny Blanchflower the previous season, but now they were cruising in 2nd place in the 2nd Division (The Championship), and favourites for promotion. Most of their glamorous 1970s team had gone; only 35-year-old Ron "Chopper" Harris remained, and he was hardly glamorous. But despite their position, their squad was pretty thin; for the Rovers game they were forced to field their inexperienced reserve goalkeeper, and play in a dreadful yellow and green strip. For Rovers, who were 18th, this was their biggest league game of the season in front of their biggest crowd. Their squad featured the likes of Gary Mabbutt, Terry Cooper, and a Tony Pulis looking for his second ever goal (he'd recently scored his first in a 1-3 QPR defeat). Shaun Penny put Rovers 1-0 ahead after 25 minutes, converting a rebound off the bar, and it could easily have been more before half-time. Then Tony lumbered forward to lob the keeper in the 56th minute, with Penny running it in (just to be sure) to claim his second. But the highlight was two minute later when Tony Pulis hit a screamer from 25 yards to make it 3-0. The crowd went mad on both sides, and with the police holding back Blues fans trying to invade the pitch, somehow the game was finished before Chelsea fans went rioting through the streets of Bristol. There was vandalism, stabbings and arrests. Within a week, dozens were in jail and banned from Chelsea for life (and that was just the players!). Tragically, Chelsea later missed out on promotion on goal-difference. If only Tony hadn't scored that goal.

Happy Valley 3 Seiko 2 – 1982
(Hong Kong Senior Challenge Shield Final)
香港高級組銀牌 Tony Pulis! 新聞稿香港高級組銀牌 Triffic final!

Fulham 1 Bournemouth 3 – Mon 4th May 1987, Att 9234

This game (unsurprisingly) superseded the Sunderland game as Tony's memorable game. (So, OK, he went through a lot of 'memorable' games.) A win at Fulham in this noon-kickoff would give Redknapp's Bournemouth promotion to the 2nd Division (The Championship) for the first time EVER. The signs looked good: Bournemouth had NEVER won at Craven Cottage, in fact apart from a couple of draws decades before, they'd always lost. So it was no surprise when Fulham got a penalty in the first half (although it was amazingly saved), and then took the lead in the second half anyway. Surely not going to be The Cherries' day. But, hell, it was Star Wars Day (MayTheFourthBeWithYou, and all that), so anything could happen. A couple of minutes later, Bournemouth equalised from the penalty spot. With 10 minutes left, Bournemouth made it 2-1, but Fulham still looked set to ruin their day. That was until the 86th minute when Tony Pulis hurled himself forward in the centre circle to win the ball. Piling forward (yes, we're talking Tony Pulis here), he laid it off to Tony Sealy who hit a brilliant unstoppable thunderbolt into the top corner to seal promotion. At the final whistle, Tony acted as cool as a cucumber; he punched the air a couple of times, hugged a couple of fans, got a couple of handshakes, applauded the huge away support, and smartly disappeared down the tunnel. Job done.

Fulham 0 Gillingham 0 – Saturday 27th April 1996, Att 10,320

Nine years later, and Tony Pulis was back at Craven Cottage to secure promotion again, this time as a manager. The aim was to win (there was an outside chance of finishing as champions), but a draw would be enough to go up this time if results went their way. Unfortunately, there was bad blood between these two sides: the previous November had seen Mark O'Connor's leg broken by a Fulham player in a bad tempered game at Priestfields, resulting in both The Gills and Fulham being charged by the FA. With Micky Adams' side struggling at the lower end of the league, failing even to get a shot on target all day, the game produced one-way traffic, with Gillingham having a goal disallowed and two penalties denied them. So when the game ended 0-0, Tony and the players went over to thank the huge away following of nearly 4,500 appreciative fans. Then the news came through: third-placed Bury had been winning 1-0 at Exeter, but late on, former-Stoke player Noel

Tony gets on TV again...

Blake had equalised from the spot and it finished 1-1. Everyone went barmy. It meant Gillingham were promoted for the first time in 22 years. The following week on May-the-4th (Star Wars Day) The Gills beat Scarborough 1-0 in front of their home crowd (it was the game that chairman Paul Scally wanted to be brought on as sub), confirming them as runners-up.....but in reality they'd been promoted straight after the Fulham game.

Gillingham 2 Manchester City 2 – 30th May 1999, Att 76,935

Imagine a wonderfully fantastic dream suddenly turning into the worst nightmare of all time. It's like that scene at the end of Raiders Of The Lost Ark, where the bad guy sees angels and says "It's beautiful!", before they instantly turn into horrific demons and blow up his head. Yep, that just about covers it. It was the 1999 2nd Division Play Off Final at Wembley. 3rd place City vs 4th place Gills – they'd been beaten to promotion by Fulham and...Walsall. Oh, the shame. Man City fans thought it couldn't get any worse – United had just secured the treble by winning the European Champions League in Barcelona 4 days before. But then at the end of a tense game, counter-attacking Carl Asaba swept into the area and blasted Gilliingham 1-0 up in the 81st minute. Asaba then set up Robert Taylor for 2-0 in the 87th, and City fans thought their world had ended, leaving the stadium in droves. For Tony Pulis, it was going to be his finest hour, an amazing win at Wembley, and promotion to the 2nd tier for the first time. The world would have been his oyster. Even when Horlock pulled one back on 90 minutes, nobody rated City's chances. But in the FIFTH minute of injury time, Dickov slipped in an equaliser for 2-2. This was the stuff of horror stories to scare teenagers round the campfire. Man City won the subsequent penalty shootout, got

Fans go on the rampage

More than 35 people were taken to hospital yesterday after Chelsea fans rampaged through Bristol after their team's 3—0 defeat by Bristol Rovers.

The fans fought running battles with police, rival fans and Saturday shoppers as they made their way from the ground to the railway station.

Shop windows were smashed, cars attacked and more than 30 fans were arrested.

Tony in the papers again

promotion, and later became multi-millionaires. Tony and his chairman fell out for the last time, and Tony's finest hour at Gillingham became his last one too. The Gills were promoted via the playoffs the following season (with mostly Tony's team). But all Tony could say after the match was "I would query how we defended." You and millions of others, mate.

Walsall 4 Stoke City 2 – Sat 2nd November 2002, Att 6,591

Famously (but unfairly) known as the "You don't know what you're doing" game. It was Tony's first game in charge of Stoke City, just 24 hours after coming aboard. The programme didn't even credit him as manager yet – it was still caretaker Dave Kevan, which was interesting as Kevan actually picked the team, not Tony. In the pouring rain, he then had to endure Walsall go 3-0 up at the start of the 2nd half. So, after taking off crowd-favourite Bjarni Gudjonsson and switching to a three-pronged attack, the 1,700 Stoke fans launched lustily into "You don't know what you're doing" as a special welcome message to Tony. What humble pie they ate when his two substitutes BOTH scored in the next 10 minutes is unclear. What is clear was that he DID know what he was doing, but some of the players clearly didn't. Defender Wayne Thomas clumsily barged his player over to concede a late penalty just as Stoke were poised to equalise. Duh. "The supporters are entitled to their views," said Tony after the game. "I know there's no money to spend and we're in a difficult position, but we're going to batten down the hatches and work 'ard to turn things around." The press were intrigued. "We can assume that this is a man, unlike some in recent times, ready to dig in and fight to the finish," reckoned a young Martin Spinks in The Sentinel. Mystic Spinksy could see everything.

Stoke City 1 Reading 0 – Sun 4th May 2003, Att 14,588

If Stoke lost (and Brighton beat already-relegated-Grimsby), then Stoke would go down to the Third Tier. This was last-chance-saloon for

Stoke and also Tony Pulis, as there was every chance that the club's Icelandic backers would have pulled the plug if that happened. So, this May-The-Fourth (yet again) game was crucial, particularly when Brighton took a 2-1 lead in their game on 47 minutes. A single goal by Reading at this stage could send Stoke down. The next 8 minutes were tense for those in the know, which must have included Tony. But then on 55 minutes, James O'Connor came out on top of a crunching tackle on the left. He released Lewis Neal whose cross was met by Ade Akinbiyi, who lost his marker and coolly headed the ball home on the run, before ripped his shirt off in an iconic moment for the fans and the TV cameras. The joy and relief were spiritual, and the crowd went crazy. They were further buoyed 5 minutes later by the news that Grimsby had equalised to make it 2-2. Surely Stoke were safe now. Only a Steve Sidwell 25 yarder that scratched the crossbar came close to threatening this. Stoke and Tony Pulis took off from here.

Stoke City 0 Leicester City 0 – Sun 4th May 2008, Att 26,609

Another May The Fourth (Star Wars Day) promotion day, but frankly not one for the faint-hearted (nor lovers of great football). No goals, but a day of infamy anyway, as Stoke were promoted on the final day of the season to the Premier League for the first time; or just back to the top flight for the first time in 23 years. As it turned out, they didn't end up needing the 0-0 draw with Leicester after all, but as it sent Mandaric's

Foxes down to the Third Division, it was job-well-done. Tony could dine out for free in Stoke for evermore. There are no reports that he ever did.

Stoke City 3 Aston Villa 2 - Sat 23rd August 2008, Att 27,500

Premier League came to The Britannia Stadium in dramatic style. PaddyPower upped the anti, paying out on bets for Stoke-to-go-down after only ONE game. But Paddy's stunt began to unravel as Tony's team hold their nerve, and a full house witness one of Stoke's greatest games, against Martin O'Neil's Top 4 wannabe. A dodgy foul on Rory Delap resulted in a Liam Lawrence penalty putting Stoke ahead. Then after an equaliser, Ricardo Fuller left Laursen for dead, and cracked in one of the Premier's goals of the season from a sharp angle for 2-1. All good stuff. But at 2-2, and in the 4th and final minute of injury time, Delap floated in a final long-throw which super-sub Mama Sidibe gently brushed his head against for the mental winner. "I don't think I will ever forget this game," gushed The Oatcake. The game became a blueprint for Stoke in the Prem.

Stoke City 5 Bolton Wanderers 0 – 17th April 2011 Att 75,064

People tuned in on their TVs to see those Stoke upstarts put in their place by the supposedly (or at least comparatively) elegant Bolton. Boy, was the watching-world in for a surprise. Bolton started the more lively, and for a few minutes it looked like Stoke might struggle on the large Wembley pitch, them being so used to a squeezed Britannia pitch. But on 11 minutes, a deflected pass landed sweetly on to Etherington's favoured left foot, and from the edge of the box he half-volleyed the ball into the left hand side of Jaaskelainen's goal. 1-0, and the Boothen End of Wembley exploded. But this was just the beginning. Six minutes later, a Wilkinson lob was headed clear, only for defender and man-mountain Huth to volley home. More erupting delirium from the red and white army behind the East goal. Now, Stoke had a history of losing FA Cup semis from 2-0 ahead, and Tony had lost at Wembley from the same position. So it was somewhat bewildering that 13 minutes later Pennant robbed Petrov of the ball on the right, and sent the mother of all through-balls to Kenwyne Jones, who calmly side-footed it home, before doing his traditional somersaults. To the strains of 'We're all going on a European tour' (3-0 meant almost certain qualification for the Europa League) Bolton were shot to pieces after the break as John Walters ran half the length of the pitch before turning inside and crashing home a 25-yard drive for 4-0. His second was a chip over several Bolton players on the line after Andy Wilkinson had come close to scoring his first ever Stoke goal only to mis-hit his shot straight to Walters with the goal gaping. There was pandemonium amongst the fans behind the goal. Even Tony Pulis could afford a smile: It was one of the best examples of his game preparation ever.

Crystal Palace 3 Liverpool 3 – Mon 5th May 2014, Att 25,261

Liverpool needed to win to have any chance of winning the League for the first time since The Stone Roses played Spike Island and Gary Lineker was the First Division's top scorer (yes, that's 1990) - even Leeds had won it more recently. Tony Pulis had played the well-what-did-you-expect-they're-millionaires card the week before at the Man City game, and many expected the same against Liverpool. Afterall, it was their last home game of the season. What was there to play for? Early on, Palace's Yannick Bolasie was lucky not to give away a penalty, but then Joe Allan headed home a Gerrard corner, much to Tony's annoyance. 0-1 at half-time, but it was the second half when things went a bit crazy. Sturridge's deflection off Delaney on 53 minutes made it 0-2, and then 2 minutes later Suarez hit his 31st Premier goal of the season. At 0-3, no one would have blamed Palace fans for leaving, not even waiting for Tony's infamously curious substitutions. For the Palace fans who stayed, it was a treat. As Liverpool pushed forward hoping to turn it into a much-needed landslide, Damien Delaney countered and got a deflected goal of his own 11 minutes from time. Then 2 minutes later, just as Liverpool had done, Palace struck again, with Bolasie squaring for super-sub Dwight Gayle to smash home for 2-3. Finally, on 88 minutes, the other super-sub Glenn Murray chested the ball into the path of Gayle for him to lash home for 3-3, with Selhurst Park going mad. At the end, Suarez wept. Crystal Palace had not only robbed Liverpool of any chance of the title, but also robbed their manager of the Premier Manager Of The Season award. Tony stole their glory from right under their noses. It's good when a plan comes together.